Ageing Issues

ISSUES

Volume 105

2 &

Editor

Craig Donnellan

Independence

Educational Publishers
Cambridge

First published by Independence
PO Box 295
Cambridge CB1 3XP
England

British Library Cataloguing in Publication Data
Ageing Issues – (Issues Series)
I. Donnellan, Craig II. Series
305.2'6

ISBN 1 86168 325 1

Printed in Great Britain
MWL Print Group Ltd

Typeset by
Lisa Firth

Cover
The illustration on the front cover is by
Simon Kneebone.

CONTENTS

Chapter One: Ageing Trends

Chapter Two: Ageism and Employment

Chapter Three: Ageing and Health

Introduction

Ageing Issues is the one hundred and fifth volume in the **Issues** series. The aim of this series is to offer up-to-date information about important issues in our world.

Ageing Issues looks at trends in ageing issues, ageism and employment, as well as ageing and health.

The information comes from a wide variety of sources and includes:
Government reports and statistics
Newspaper reports and features
Magazine articles and surveys
Website material
Literature from lobby groups
and charitable organisations.

It is hoped that, as you read about the many aspects of the issues explored in this book, you will critically evaluate the information presented. It is important that you decide whether you are being presented with facts or opinions. Does the writer give a biased or an unbiased report? If an opinion is being expressed, do you agree with the writer?

Ageing Issues offers a useful starting-point for those who need convenient access to information about the many issues involved. However, it is only a starting-point. At the back of the book is a list of organisations which you may want to contact for further information.

*****

Ageing

Frequently asked questions

'If I'd known I was gonna live this long, I'd have taken more care of myself' – Eubie Blake, Jazz Musician, on reaching 100.

Ageing affects us all, so most of us have questions about it. What exactly is ageing? Why have lifespans increased so dramatically? What can I do to age successfully? This article answers the questions we are most often asked. You may find some of the answers surprising – we hope you will find them interesting and useful.

What is ageing?

One morning we look in the mirror and notice a little clutch of grey hairs or that the skin round the eyes appears to be sagging. We have all been there. Why, for goodness' sake, and why now?

One of the best solutions to this difficult question was provided by Professor Tom Kirkwood. After years of studying ageing, he had one of those 'eureka' moments which he realised after years of studying ageing by focusing on our bodies' cells. He

realised that we age because only our genes need to survive. The rest of us is disposable. That sounds brutal but it is a very neat solution to a biological problem.

Tom explains his theory thus: 'The problem is this. Life is inherently risky. For our evolutionary ancestors life was much riskier than it is today. At any time they might be over-whelmed by infection, illness, accident, or starvation.

'How to make sure that, despite the risks, the species nonetheless survives? The answer evolution came up with was to invest more high quality protection mechanisms in the sex cells, which carry the genes to the next generation, but to invest less in the protection of other – non-sex – cells.

'These other non-sex cells – the somatic cells – are needed only for as long as we manage to stay alive. Before the increases in life expectancy of the last 200 years, most people could only expect to live about 30 years on average and it was rare to live past 60. So our genes settled

for less than perfect repair of somatic cells – and that is why we age.

'What is extraordinary about our cells, however, is that although the programming for survival is not perfect, it is incredibly good. We eventually suffer from frailty and age-related disease because, over the decades, a host of tiny faults accumulates in our cells. But these faults, which arise as accidental by-products of the chemistry of life, would build up very much faster if we were not protected by fantastic cellular repair systems.

'This theory offers good news. By studying how to support the repair and maintenance functions of the cell, we can do much to improve how we age and to ensure that we live as long as possible free of the disabling conditions that can under-mine our quality of later life.'

Research Into Ageing, a special trust within Help the Aged, is working to improve the under-standing and treatment of illness in old age. We raise money to fund investigations into conditions like stroke, dementia, mobility problems and osteoporosis. To learn more about the projects Research Into Ageing funds visit www.ageing.org. To donate directly to their work please see www.helptheaged.org.uk/SupportUs/_riadonate.htm.

Why has our life expectancy increased?

In the twentieth century average life expectancy is continuing to increase by over 20 years in the UK and many other developed countries, and our lifespans are continuing to increase. Many factors have contributed to this phenomenal success story.

Higher living standards and better public health have played key roles. Today we have better diets than our

ancestors of just a century ago, with the result that our immune systems are in better shape to withstand infections like bronchitis and influenza that previously caused many early deaths. We no longer live in overcrowded, damp or unsanitary housing where disease was common and easily spread.

We now have safe, clean drinking water, proper sanitation and much higher standards of hygiene in public places and the home. These measures have helped eliminate preventable illnesses like typhoid, cholera and dysentery. Although air pollution is still a major health issue, our air is much cleaner than it was a century ago when factory chimneys and domestic fires belched smoke and gave rise to chronic chest problems in a high proportion of the population.

Medical science has also made a major contribution. The twentieth century saw the big breakthroughs in vaccination and immunisation, with the result that killer diseases of childhood like diphtheria, tuberculosis and polio were held in check. Smallpox became the first disease to be eliminated altogether by an international programme of vaccination. The development of antibiotics gave the first effective treatment against other serious infections, enabling people to survive illnesses like pneumonia. Better medical care has also meant that few women now die in childbirth and it has dramatically improved the life chances of small or premature babies.

The significance of all these advances is that they have enabled more people than ever before to survive the rigours of childhood and young adulthood. Of a million babies born in England and Wales in the 1880s, more than a quarter (263,000) died before their fifth birthday, and just over half were still alive at 35. It was these early deaths that kept average life expectancy so low. Of a million babies born in the 1990s, more than four-fifths (831,000) will still be alive at 65, so average life expectancy is much higher. Following implementation of measures derived from population studies, the epidemic of heart disease has now been halted and in some developed

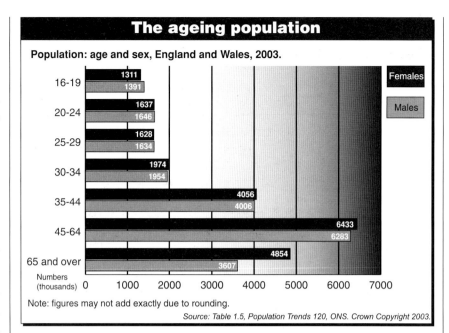

The ageing population

Population: age and sex, England and Wales, 2003.

Age	Females	Males
16-19	1311	1391
20-24	1637	1646
25-29	1628	1634
30-34	1974	1954
35-44	4056	4006
45-64	6433	6283
65 and over	4854	3607

Numbers (thousands): 0 1000 2000 3000 4000 5000 6000 7000

Note: figures may not add exactly due to rounding.

Source: Table 1.5, Population Trends 120, ONS. Crown Copyright 2003.

countries has now fallen substantially. However, in developing countries, it is continuing to increase.

Why do women live longer than men?

Women do indeed live longer than men in most countries of the world. In the UK in 2002, life expectancy, at birth, was 74 for men, whereas it was 81 for women, a difference of seven years. The figures for other developed countries are broadly similar. By 2031 it's expected to rise to 81 for men and 84.9 for women.

In a few countries, like Bangladesh for instance, men live slightly longer than women (with a life expectancy of 57 and 56 respectively), but such places are now the exception. The reason women have shorter lives in countries like Bangladesh is due to the lack of investment in women's health and particularly in maternal health.

There are two answers to the puzzle as to why women last the distance better than men do. Life-

style plays a very important role in our life expectancy, and men often make unhealthy choices. Men are more likely than women to smoke, with the result that more die before their time of lung cancer, other smoking-related cancers, and heart disease.

Excessive intake of alcohol is a factor in men's premature deaths in some societies, while in many industrialised countries deaths from occupational causes inflict a greater toll on men than on women. It may also be true that women are physically more active throughout life; women do more of the 'physiotherapy of daily living', such as getting the shopping in and doing the housework, and exercise protects against many age-related conditions.

But there are also biological answers. There is growing evidence that women are biologically tougher than men. For example, we now know that female hormones protect women from heart disease, at least until the menopause. The reasons for women's biological resilience have to do with the way we have all evolved to play our reproductive roles.

Our genes stand a better chance of survival if the nurturing parent – the mother – survives to care for her offspring until they are able to fend for themselves. In biological terms, men are expendable at younger ages because their genetic investment does not depend on their personal survival.

How healthy are older people in the UK?

This is a surprisingly difficult question to answer due to a shortage of national information on our state of health. We do know a great deal about the prevalence of specific disorders, stroke for example, becomes more common with age. Three out of four strokes occur in people over the age of 65, and the incidence rises with increasing age.

However, it is easy from these studies to view older generations as unhealthy and even downright decrepit. The truth is more complex. The 2000 General Household Survey, carried out by the Office for National Statistics, asks some helpful questions about the ability of people over 65 to do basic tasks, from which we know that:

- 91 per cent can get around the house with no difficulty;
- 72 per cent can get up and down stairs with no difficulty;
- 77 per cent can get out and about on their own with no difficulty.

These figures imply a fairly fit and active older population. We also know from studies of particular diseases that most older people enjoy good mental health too. To turn the usual statistics on their heads:

- 95 per cent of people aged between 70 and 80 are unaffected by dementia;
- 80 per cent of those aged 80-90 do not have dementia;

- 66 per cent of those aged 90 plus are free of dementia;
- 85-90 per cent of people over 65 do not suffer from depression.

What the statistics do show is a considerable difference between the health of 'young elderly' people in their 60s, and that of their own parents' generation in their 80s and 90s. 'Young elderly' people are remarkably fit; many of our business leaders, politicians, entertainers and writers belong to this cohort, as do a high proportion of users of the Internet! Their parents are the generation most at risk of age-related conditions like heart disease, stroke, cancer, arthritis, dementia, and disabling sensory losses, especially deafness but also impaired sight. The good news is that illness and disability tend to be compressed into a few short years at the end of our long lives, and one of the aims of Research Into Ageing is to reduce this period still further.

Will older people be fitter in the future?

In all probability, yes. It is difficult to look to the future with total certainty. Current trends towards healthier lives may be blown off course by unpredictable factors such as major economic recession (there is a powerful link between poverty and ill health) or the fashion for smoking, to give just two examples. The numbers of people who smoke have

been in steady decline in the past decades, but if that single trend were to be reversed, we could expect to see a worsening of the nation's health.

But with these provisos in mind, the future does look very promising. First, there is considerable scope to prevent some of the disabling conditions of later life. Stroke and osteoporosis (thinning of the bones) are two good examples. Stroke can be prevented by controlling blood pressure and reducing smoking. Osteoporosis affects women more commonly than men and can be held in check by hormone replacement therapy, exercise and higher intake of calcium and vitamin D.

Second, there is every likelihood that the next few decades will see major breakthroughs in treating some common conditions. There is currently no treatment for acute stroke, though careful management of the condition in special stroke units dramatically increases the chance of survival. But the race is on to find effective treatments for acute stroke, some of them funded by Research Into Ageing, and the next decade may produce real advances. Sound biomedical research is likely to yield similar dividends for conditions as diverse as heart disease, some cancers and Alzheimer's disease.

Third, we have unravelled the human genetic code. This understanding will undoubtedly pave the way for further advances in the prevention and treatment of many illnesses.

Whatever the outcomes of science, our future health is, to a large extent, in our own hands. Most preventive strategies will only work if we are receptive to health messages. A healthy lifestyle is a prerequisite for a healthier old age.

- The above information is an extract from information supplied by Help the Aged and reprinted with permission – for more information or to view the entire text, please visit www.helptheaged.org.uk, or if you wish to write to them to request information, see page 41 for address details.

© Help the Aged

Older people in the United Kingdom

General statistics 2004

In the United Kingdom, in 2003, according to estimates based on the 2001 Census of Population, there were over 11 million older people (11,014,000):

- 9,190,000 in England
- 958,000 in Scotland
- 596,000 in Wales
- 271,000 in Northern Ireland.

82% of those aged 65 and over voted at the 2001 General Election compared to 43% of those aged 18-24.

An ageing population

In 2003, the population of the United Kingdom, based on mid-year estimates, was 59,554,000. Of this figure, 18.5% were over pensionable age:

- 6,976,000 were women aged 60 and over (of whom 5,472,000 were aged 65 and over)
- 4,038,000 were men aged 65 and over
- 9,510,000 were people aged 65 and over
- 4,505,000 were people aged 75 and over
- 1,104,000 were people aged 85 and over

In 2002 a man of 60 could expect to live for another 20 years and a woman of the same age for 23.3 years (figures may be subject to further revision)

In mid-2001, in the United Kingdom, 8,100 people were estimated to be aged 100 and over.

Looking at the ethnic minority population in the United Kingdom, in 2001, within specific groups:

- 11% of Black-Caribbean people were aged over 65
- 2% of Black-African people were aged over 65
- 7% of Indian people were aged over 65
- 4% of Pakistani people were aged over 65
- 3% of Bangladeshi people were aged over 65
- 5% of Chinese people were aged over 65.

An ageing population in the future

The number of people over pensionable age, taking account of the change in the women's retirement age, is projected to increase from nearly 11.4 million in 2006 to 12.2 million in 2011, and will rise to nearly 13.9 million by 2026, reaching over 15.2 million in 2031.

Employment

In 2004 over 6 million people aged between 50 and the State Pension Age are in employment. The employment rate for men between the ages of 50 and 64 is 71.9%, and for women between the ages of 50 and 59 is 67.9%. This compares to an employment rate for all people of working age of 74.7%.

In mid-2001, in the United Kingdom, 8,100 people were estimated to be aged 100 and over

In Spring 2004, 8.5% of men aged 65 and over and 9.9% of women aged 60 and over were still in employment.

Income

The basic pension from April 2004 to April 2005 is £79.60 for a single pensioner and £127.25 for a couple (claiming on the husband's contributions) per week.

In 2002-03, single pensioners received, on average, £177 net income per week. Pensioner couples received £327 per week on average for the same period.

Older pensioner households have lower incomes. In 2002-03 pensioner couples where the man was aged 75 and over received £292 net income per week on average, compared with £346 net income per week for those aged under 75.

17% of single older men and 21% of single older women are in poverty.

Poverty is defined as living in a household where the income is less than 60 per cent of the median income of the population as a whole.

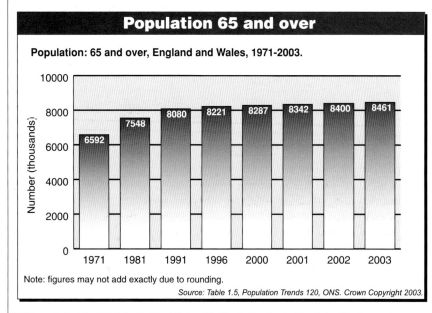

Population 65 and over

Population: 65 and over, England and Wales, 1971-2003.

Year	Number (thousands)
1971	6592
1981	7548
1991	8080
1996	8221
2000	8287
2001	8342
2002	8400
2003	8461

Note: figures may not add exactly due to rounding.

Source: Table 1.5, Population Trends 120, ONS. Crown Copyright 2003.

In 2002-03, 69% of pensioner households depended on state benefits for at least 50% of their income.

The Department for Work and Pensions estimates that, in 2001-02, between 28% and 37% of pensioners who were entitled to Minimum Income Guarantee, between 10% and 17% who were entitled to Housing Benefit, and between 37% and 43% entitled to Council Tax Benefit, did not claim.

Minimum Income Guarantee was replaced by Pension Credit in October 2003.

In September 2004, the number of pensioner households receiving Pension Credit was 2.62 million (3.18 million individuals). Around 3.75 million households are estimated to be eligible for Pension Credit.

Pension Credit replaced Minimum Income Guarantee in October 2003.

Spending

Where the head of the household is aged 65 and over, a higher proportion of money is spent on housing, fuel and food (28% of expenditure) than in other households (20%).

The most severe deprivation is experienced by pensioners living alone who are mainly dependent on state pensions: 41.9% of their expenditure goes on housing, fuel and food.

In 2002-03, one-adult retired households mainly dependent on state pensions spent £19.60 per week on food, compared with £21.30 for single non-retired households (the commodity and service categories are not comparable with those in publications before 2001-02).

In 2002-03, of pensioners mainly dependent on state pensions and living alone:

- 88% had central heating, compared to 93% of all households
- 16% had a car, compared to 77% of all households
- 14% had a mobile phone, compared to 84% of all households
- 74% had a washing machine, compared to 96% of all households
- 35% had a CD player, compared to 92% of all households ('all households' relates to households without children).

Living alone

In 2002, in the 65-74 age group, 18% of men and 34% of women lived alone, and 29% of men and 60% of women aged 75 and over lived alone.

In 2002 the likelihood of living alone increased with age, with 48% of those aged 75 and over living alone, compared with 12% of those aged 25-44.

In 2002, of people aged 65 to 74:

- 76% of men were married
- 58% of women were married
- 9% of men were widowed
- 28% of women were widowed.
Of people aged 75 and over:
- 63% of men were married
- 28% of women were married
- 28% of men were widowed
- 62% of women were widowed.

Leisure, learning and computers

In 2002, 33% of households with two adults, one or both aged 60 or over, and 9% of single-person households aged 60 or over owned a home computer.

Where the head of the household is aged 65 and over, a higher proportion of money is spent on housing, fuel and food (28% of expenditure) than in other households (20%)

In 2002, 27% of households with two adults, one or both aged 60 or over, and 6% of single-person households aged 60 or over, had access to the internet at home.

In 2004, 14% of people aged 65-74, and 10% of people aged 75 and over, took part in some sort of adult learning.

In 2002, walking was the most popular physical activity for older people, with 39% of men and 35% of women aged 60-69, 27% of men and 18% of women aged 70-79, engaging in a walk of two miles or over in the four weeks before interview.

In 2002, of those interviewed for the General Household Survey, 99% of those aged 60-69 and 99% of those aged 70 and over had watched

television during the previous month. The next most popular home-based leisure activity was listening to the radio (82% and 76%), followed by listening to records/tapes (71% and 57%).

The safety and health of older people

In 2002, 63% of people aged 65-74 and 72% of people aged 75 and over in the GHS sample reported a longstanding illness. Of those aged between 65 and 74, 41% and, of those aged 75 and over, 53% said that they had a limiting longstanding illness.

The Alzheimer's Society estimates that there are currently over 750,000 people in the UK with dementia, of which only 18,000 are aged under 65.

In 2002, in England and Wales, the deaths of 71 people aged 65 and over involved hypothermia as the underlying cause, according to their death certificates.

In the winter of 2003/2004, 21,500 people over the age of 65 died as a result of the cold in England and Wales.

Excess winter mortality is defined as deaths occurring in December-March minus the average of the deaths in the preceding August to November and the following April to July.

In 2002, 19% of all accidents within the home involved people aged 65 and over.

In 2003, of 774 pedestrian fatalities on the road, 307 (39.7%) were people aged 60 and over.

Housing

In England, during 2003:

- 56% of owner occupiers without a mortgage were 65 and over
- 3% of owner occupiers with a mortgage were 65 and over
- 35% of those renting from local authorities were 65 and over
- 32% of those renting from housing associations were 65 and over
- 11% of those renting privately were 65 or over.

In 2001, in England, some 2.4 million 'older' households with at least one person aged 60 years or more lived in non-decent homes (comprising 36% of all households in non-decent homes). Of these, 734,000 are aged 75-84 and a further 275,000 are aged 85 or more. Some 29% of older households required work to improve the thermal comfort of their homes compared with 24% of other households.

In 2001, 4% of people aged 65-69, 7% of people aged 70-74, 10% of people aged 75-79, 13% of people aged 80-84 and 19% of people aged 85 and over lived in sheltered accommodation.

In April 2004, in the United Kingdom, there were an estimated 13,176 registered care homes for older people. There were an estimated 486,000 places for the nursing, residential (personal) and long-stay hospital care of older, chronically ill and physically disabled people (with regard to numbers of older people in residential and nursing homes, it should be noted that statistics relate to the primary purpose of the home rather than to the individuals within them).

In 2004 the chance of living in a long-stay hospital or care home by age was:

- 0.9% (65-74)
- 4.3% (75-84)
- 20.7% (85 plus).

Health and social care services

In 2002, in a three-month period, 25% of those aged 75 and over had attended the casualty or out-patient department of a hospital, compared with 14% of people of all ages.

In 2002, of those admitted to hospital in the previous 12 months, the average stay was 7 nights. However, those aged 75 and over spent, on average, 12 nights.

In 2002, 86% of NHS GP consultations took place in the surgery. Consultations at home were most likely for older people, with 17% of consultations for those aged 75 and over being at home.

In England, from 1 April 2002 to 31 March 2003, 479,000 clients over the age of 65 received home help or home care services, 157,000 received day care and 189,000 received meals.

In England and Wales, in 2001, 342,032 people aged 65 and over provided 50 hours or more of unpaid care per week.

- Information from Age Concern. To view data sources, please visit www.ace.org.uk/AgeConcern/information_2662.htm, or see page 41 for their address details.

© Age Concern

Male over fifties, reliving the swinging sixties

Information from Mintel

Latest research from Mintel introduces generation SYLO, heralding a new way of life for today's over fifties. Generation SYLO are Staying Younger LOnger by refusing to succumb to the image of the older consumer associated with their parents' generation.

In particular, British men over fifty are refusing to let go of the swinging sixties. These men were the original teenagers and the legacy of the 1960s has remained with them. They have become today's ageing, denim-wearing rockers, who have a strong sense of duty and ethical awareness. And while the women of their generation take real care of their appearance, SYLO men have a more chilled-out attitude to their maturing looks and simply wait for women to fall at their feet.

Gyrating Jaggers – the ageing rocker?

For almost half of men over 50, music is still an important part of life. Amazingly at this stage in life, men are just as likely to go to pop and rock concerts as they are to go to classical music concerts and recitals (15%). These are far more popular than jazz concerts (10%) and operas (7%). In fact among the 50-54 year olds pop and rock concerts are by far and away the most popular type of concert, with one in four (24%) dancing the night away.

What is more, men over fifty are doing their best to keep up with today's changing music world, as an impressive one in four (26%) have downloaded music or videos from the Internet.

Generation SYLO are Staying Younger LOnger by refusing to succumb to the image of the older consumer associated with their parents' generation

'This generation has grown up with many different forms of popular music and a continuing interest in the music they listened to in their youth is a feature of middle-aged life for many people. With many artists who made their names in the 1960s and 1970s still performing regularly, as well as the emergence of tribute bands, there are numerous opportunities for them to re-live their youth at concerts,' comments Angela Hughes, Consumer Research Manager at Mintel.

At this age, it is the men who wear the jeans, with two in five doing so, compared to just over one in four (27%) women. Women let their denims go a lot younger than men, discarding their jeans at around their mid-fifties, while men hold onto them until their mid-sixties. That said, this does not necessarily mean that men are more fashionable than women. Indeed fewer than one in ten (8%) men of this age say that they only buy fashionable clothes, compared to double the number of women (18%) of the same age.

'The lack of interest among men is probably partly to do with the fact that fewer men of their generation were interested in their appearance, even when they were younger. But jeans have always been associated with youth culture and rebellion and these men seem reluctant to give this up,' comments Angela Hughes.

Striving to be the scruffy sex symbols

At this age men are more likely than women to feel that it is important to be attractive to the opposite sex, with almost two in five men (38%) feeling this way, compared to three in ten

(31%) women. Ironically, while men may feel it is important to be attractive to women, they seem reluctant to look after their image. Only just over half (52%) of men of this age look after their appearance and image, compared to some 70% of women, which suggests an air of self-confidence about them.

'Men should not be resting on their laurels. It may be that men used to mature better than women, but women today are taking greater care of their health and appearance with help from a wealth of new products and services. With women taking more of an interest in the way they look, can men really afford to do nothing about their appearance for

much longer and still expect women to find them attractive?' questions Angela Hughes.

Amongst divorced men of this age, being perceived as attractive becomes even more important, as almost half recognise the importance of looking good. By contrast attracting the opposite sex decreases amongst divorced women, which suggests that men are keen to find another partner, while women look to become more self-sufficient. Women seem more content with a network of friends and family rather than a new relationship.

Overall, adults in their sixties and seventies are just as likely as those in their thirties and forties to say that they look after their appearance, at over 60%. Although those in their 20s are the most likely to see the importance in the way they look and are dressed, once people hit thirty their attitudes become very stabilised.

Budding Bobs (Geldof)

Men of this older generation – particularly those over 70 – have a more highly developed sense of duty than those who are younger. Over half (55%) of men over 70 and almost four in ten (36%) men aged 50-69 agree that 'it is more important to do your duty than to live for your own enjoyment'. This is compared to fewer than one in five of those under 50 years old.

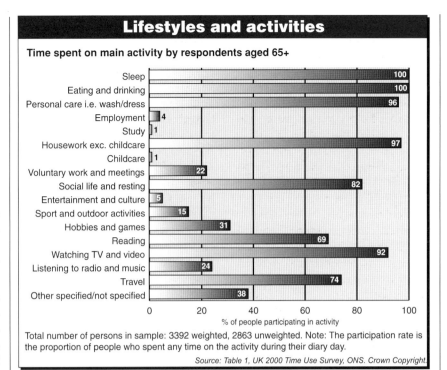

Lifestyles and activities

Time spent on main activity by respondents aged 65+

Activity	%
Sleep	100
Eating and drinking	100
Personal care i.e. wash/dress	96
Employment	4
Study	1
Housework exc. childcare	97
Childcare	1
Voluntary work and meetings	22
Social life and resting	82
Entertainment and culture	5
Sport and outdoor activities	15
Hobbies and games	31
Reading	69
Watching TV and video	92
Listening to radio and music	24
Travel	74
Other specified/not specified	38

% of people participating in activity

Total number of persons in sample: 3392 weighted, 2863 unweighted. Note: The participation rate is the proportion of people who spent any time on the activity during their diary day.

Source: Table 1, UK 2000 Time Use Survey, ONS. Crown Copyright.

This group of wannabe Bob Geldofs are particularly concerned about ethical consumerism. Around two-thirds (63%) of 50- to 69-year-old men feel that it is important that a company acts ethically.

Happy hippies have found peace and harmony

Today, men in their fifties and sixties have adopted a more carefree attitude towards the way they live their lives, as some two in five (40%) claim to 'enjoy life and not worry about the future'. Interestingly, adults in their twenties are no more likely to feel this way than these laid back over-fifty-year-olds.

What is more, two-thirds (66%) of men of this age are 'very happy with their life as it is', with this contentment rising with age. This is compared to just 58% amongst the 15- to 29-year-old adults.

'For many, the best thing about being over 50 can be summed up in one word: Freedom. This may be freedom from work, from family responsibilities and financial worries,' explains Angela Hughes.

The chilled-out approach to life has remained with these male sixties throwbacks throughout their family years and so when it comes to time management today, they seem considerably more laid back than other generations. Almost one in five (18%) men say that they 'cannot see the point in rushing around and avoid it as much as possible', compared to just 14% of the population as a whole.

I get by with a little help from my friends

At this age having 'close friends they can rely on' is the most important thing in life, with almost half (48%) of 50- to 69-year-olds selecting this as a top 3 priority. This comes some way ahead of making sure that they are secure financially in the long term (35%). Getting married, living with a partner or being in a steady relationship also follow some way behind.

Looking out for themselves is also important, with one in four (23%) saying having good holidays is most important, along with a further 14% who want enough money to spend

on themselves, and almost one in ten (8%) stating going out and having a good social life.

Silver surfers

Almost half of those adults in their fifties (45%) and one in three in their sixties (34%) say that they try to keep up with developments in technology. Men (52%) are far more likely than women (29%) to feel this way, and one in four men of this age use the Internet at home several times a day. Among adults aged 50- to 69-years-old with Internet access at home, the majority have sent and received emails, browsed or used a search engine for information. This is true even of those in the 60 to 69 age group. Reunion sites are also popular as one in three (29%) 50- to 69-year-old male Internet users have visited one, perhaps looking for an old flame.

'The potential of new technology, particularly the Internet, for this age group has already been recognised, and the phenomenon of the silver surfer is now well established. The over fifties are clearly keen to embrace the concept of life-long learning, and acquiring new skills is a favourite way of using the increased free time that many find themselves with at this time of life,' comments Angela Hughes.

■ The above information is from Mintel's website and can be found at http://reports.mintel.com

© Mintel

The young worry more about getting older

Information from Age Concern

A national survey has found that younger people worry more about getting older than older people do. This startling difference in opinion was one of many which emerged out of the research, which surveyed over 2,000 people, challenging some mainstream views about the young and their relationship with the older generation.

According to the Mature Market, the so-called 'Selfish Generation' was found to be not so selfish when it came to their parents, with two-thirds saying they expect to take care of the parents when they get older. 29 per cent want their parents to live with them.

In stark contrast, only 12 per cent of people over 65 in the survey said they want to live with their children, while only 28 per cent expect their children to take care of them, preferring to keep their independence as long as possible.

Older people were more positive about getting old, with financial considerations less important and most feeling they would not miss out on anything in old age.

Younger people, however, generally cited stronger concerns about getting older. Younger men were more worried about financially supporting themselves after retirement, while younger women were more worried about being lonely.

Both younger and older generations were unified on the front that they are dissatisfied with the government's treatment of older people, and that older people's issues are not high enough on the political agenda.

■ The above information is from Age Concern's website which can be found at www.ace.org.uk, or see page 41 for their address details.

© DeHavilland Information Services plc

The gender gap

In the UK, the gap between male and female lifespans stands at just over four years, with women living to an average of 79 and men 75

This male/female divide exists worldwide, and in some countries it's a lot more marked. In Russia, for example, life expectancy is 66.4 years for women, but a depressing 56 for men.

Not only is life expectancy increasing generally and predicted to continue to do so, but the gender gap appears to narrow as people get older. So are women as a rule programmed to live longer than their male counterparts? Or can men achieve equality of lifespan by making changes to their lifestyles? The answer, predictably perhaps, is yes to both. Women do have some inbuilt biological advantages, but there is still a lot men can do to improve the odds of living longer.

Survive youth – and live long

'The most important piece of advice you can give men is to stay alive while they're young!' says Jim Pollard, editor of the men's health resource website www.malehealth.co.uk. 'Death rates among young men remain high because of suicide, accident and HIV. But the further you get down the road, the better your likelihood of living a bit longer. The fact that you're still alive [beyond

SAGAmagazine

your youth] means your life expectancy isn't much different from that of females.'

This view is borne out by statistics gathered by the Faculty and Institute of Actuaries in 1999. According to the figures, which are based on insurance data, male longevity is improving more rapidly than the female rate. The chance of 50- to 60-year-old men dying has fallen by up to 35 per cent – a reduction thought to result from medical advances and a decline in the number of male smokers.

What you can do: stop smoking; ask your doctor about treatments that can help if you can't manage it on your own.

Biological factors

Certainly, biological factors play their part in determining lifespan. Men don't have the hormone oestrogen to protect them from heart disease, while testosterone (which they do have, in significant amounts) may play a part in raising cholesterol

levels and thereby increasing the risk of heart problems. Coronary heart disease is the single biggest killer of men, affecting one in four males but only one in six women. And there is also new evidence to suggest that men's immune systems may function inherently less efficiently than women's.

What you can do: eat a healthy diet, try to avoid saturated fats as far as possible and take steps to boost your immune system. To find out how, please visit our website at www.saga.co.uk

Changing lifestyles and attitudes

But some of the causes of the health gender gap are lifestyle-related too. In Russia, for example, the reason men are dying so young is mainly put down to alcohol abuse. British men drink too much too, and around 45 per cent of them are overweight.

Perhaps one of the major factors in men's relatively shorter lives lies in the way in which they approach their health and access medical facilities. Men are less likely than women to visit the GP. They don't tend to talk about their health and, as they don't get pregnant or have periods, they aren't perhaps as in touch with their bodies as women and don't have the routine contact with health services that women do.

Again, though, this disparity narrows as people grow older. 'Just as, hormonally, older men and older women grow more alike, so mentally older men become more feminine in their attitudes to health,' says Pollard.

What you can do: limit your drinking to a maximum of 21 units a week – spread out over seven days not all at once! Don't put off visiting the doctor when you have unexplained symptoms and, if you need help to lose weight, ask your doctor's advice.

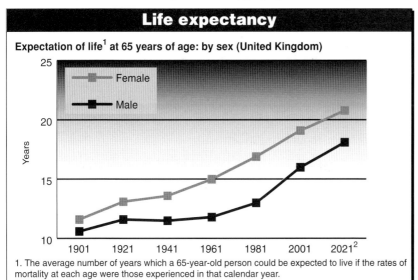

Life expectancy

Expectation of life[1] at 65 years of age: by sex (United Kingdom)

1. The average number of years which a 65-year-old person could be expected to live if the rates of mortality at each age were those experienced in that calendar year.
2. 2001-based projections.
Source: Government Actuary's Department. Figure 7.1, Social Trends 33. Crown Copyright.

Look after yourself

Stress also has a part to play in men's shorter lifespan. 'One of the things that kills men is working. Research shows that people who work long hours for a long period of time will die younger than people who work more reasonable hours,' says Pollard.

The death rates from heart disease have fallen by 10 per cent in the last two years, partly because of lifestyle changes and partly because of improved treatments and surgical techniques. However, the rates would probably drop still further if men were to make some simple lifestyle changes. 'In terms of diet, men seem to take in more salt than women and that pushes their blood pressure up,' says Craig Haslop, spokesman for the British Heart Foundation. 'A lower salt intake is important to fight heart disease.'

What you can do: to reduce your risk of heart disease, take 30 minutes of exercise five times a week and eat five portions of fruit and vegetables a day. Talking about your problems instead of bottling them up can ease stress and remember that you need to look after yourself, especially after a lifetime of working.

Men's health in general is years and years behind women's. Most men still know more about breast cancer than they do about prostate cancer

---

More resources

The lack of attention given to men's health as a specific issue may also contribute to the gender gap. Prostate cancer is a case in point. It's one of the major killers of men, affecting around 21,000 British men per year and killing 10,000. That compares to the 13,000 women killed by breast cancer, yet prostate cancer remains relatively low profile.

'The major difference is that women have fought to get breast cancer into the public eye, whereas men are not so open and forthcoming in talking about their health in general,' says Katie Easter, press and PR officer for the Prostate Cancer Charity. 'Also, the media tend to be quite ageist and, although there are cases affecting 40-year-olds and upwards, prostate cancer generally affects men over 60.'

There are causes for optimism, however. 'Things are changing,' says Easter. 'Men are becoming more aware of health issues, particularly the younger generation. There are men's charities out there and they are making an impact, but men's health in general is years and years behind women's. Most men still know more about breast cancer than they do about prostate cancer.'

■ The above information is reprinted with permission from Saga Health – visit www.saga.co.uk for more information.

© SAGA

New phones help to keep elderly mobile

The elderly can now buy mobile telephones specially adapted for their needs, among them 'childlike simplicity' and instant connection to a medical call centre.

They offer functions slightly more relevant to the autumn years, such as on-the-spot cardiograms or GPS navigation to plot its location

---

By Kate Connolly in Berlin

The new models do not send text messages, take photographs or download ringtones. Instead they offer functions slightly more relevant to the autumn years, such as on-the-spot cardiograms or GPS navigation to plot its location if, say, grandpa or granny get lost.

One, the Vitaphone 1100, is an elderly technophobe's dream, having just three buttons. The red one connects the owner to a medical centre with doctors ready to deliver instant diagnoses by telephone or send ambulances to the rescue.

'Green' and 'yellow' can be programmed to dial two emergency numbers, a favourite daughter or the family doctor, for example.

The telephone has extra long-life batteries so that even if the owner forgets to plug it in to recharge, it will work for more than 100 hours. It can also be worn round the neck to ensure that it is always at hand.

Priced at around £60, the 1100 is currently being sold on a trial basis in selected chemists across Germany.

Elderly people on the move will be able to communicate their precise

location at the touch of a button or to obtain instant cardiograms if they suspect that they are having a heart attack, courtesy of the Vitaphone 2300, available in German-speaking countries from £25 a month.

According to Benjamin Homberg of Vitaphone lives have already been saved by the cardiogram telephone, known as the 'Herz Handy', or 'heart mobile'.

He said: 'Already emergency calls have been received from people with suspected heart problems. In four cases they were heart attacks, in three cases life-threatening irregular heart rhythms. We even had a case of a man climbing on Mont Blanc who had to be rushed to hospital after an ECG showed things were not looking good.'

The telephones have so far proved to be very popular with people recovering from heart attacks or surgery. 'Your doctor tells you to go out and exercise every day, but most people find this a scary prospect, and are reluctant to go further than the bottom of the garden,' said Mr Homberg. 'Now they have much more freedom.'

Telephones held close to the heart send signals and the precise satellite position of the patient back to the medical centre in Chemnitz, eastern Germany, where doctors assess the problem.

Older consumers had been largely ignored by the youth-focused mobile telephone market, Mr Homberg said. 'Everyone has their own needs but in this case older people are less interested in sending text messages, but more interested in knowing that they can contact relatives or a doctor.'

Older people are less interested in sending text messages, but more interested in knowing that they can contact relatives or a doctor

---

The telephones were launched in Hanover at the CeBIT technology fair.

The company said the handsets were ideal for people wanting to keep track of their elderly relatives – even if they were holidaying in a different continent.

© *Telegraph Group Limited, London 2005*

According to research by Tesco Telecoms, more pensioners have taken up using the Internet than any other age group. People over 60 are learning to use the Internet, email and generally becoming more computer savvy.

The survey found that 56 per cent of respondents used email to keep in touch with their grandchildren. They noted that this was the only way they were able to keep in constant contact with them.

It also found that OAPs are using the net to make new friends by using chat rooms, one in four saying they use this service.

Internet spending is also big. The survey found that shopping online was utilised by people who found it hard to go to the shops and carry bags.

'It's exciting to see that the fastest growing sector of Internet users is those over the age of 60,' said Andy Dewhurst, CEO of Tesco telecoms.

'Email is a great way of staying in touch and keeping up with all the latest gossip so it's no surprise that the older generation are continuing the trend to get net savvy.'

■ The above information is from Age Concern – visit www.ace.org.uk for more information or see page 41 for address details.

© *DeHavilland Information Services plc*

Britain's old and lonely

New survey reveals more than 1.28 million older people feel lonely and 250,000 have no family or friends

A new survey conducted by NOP World released today (31 March 2005) from Help the Aged reveals the true extent of loneliness amongst older people in the UK with 1.28 million (14 per cent) feeling lonely.*

The survey findings come as the charity launches a new national awareness and fundraising campaign running throughout April called Helping Unite Generations (Hug), which aims to help end loneliness among older people.

It appears that as lives get busier there is less time to visit older relatives. One in ten (11 per cent) of older people see their grandchildren less than twice a year; 19 per cent of those who live alone will go more than a month without seeing any members of their family, and 9 per cent will go more than six months.

> **19% of those who live alone will go more than a month without seeing any members of their family, and 9% will go more than six months**

Feelings of loneliness can be even more acute during traditional holiday times such as Christmas and Easter, which are associated with cosy images of families spending time together. Staggeringly, more than 1 million older people (11 per cent) spent last Christmas Day alone.

Paul Cann, Director of Policy at Help the Aged, said: 'The findings of this survey make depressing reading. We far too often shunt older people into the sidings of life, leaving them without enough money, activity but above all human warmth. Our Hug campaign is important because in addition to raising funds to help with practical solutions, it also aims to unite generations and challenges all our families, friends and neighbours to bring our oldest and frailest citizens in from the cold of our indifference and neglect.'

Other findings from the survey were:

- More than 3 million older people (36 per cent) feel out of touch with the fast pace of modern life
- 820,000 (9 per cent) feel cut off from society
- Nearly 2 million (21 per cent) do not feel valued as an older member of society.

The survey also explores older people's contact with the younger generation:

- More than 68 per cent of older people do not have any friends under the age of 30 whom they visit or are visited by
- However, more than 2 million older people (23 per cent) would generally like to have more social contact with younger people.

Paul Cann added: 'You can help make a difference and get involved in Hug Month during April by hosting your own Hug Quiz. You can also buy purple Hug badges and a specially designed wristband from Help the Aged shops and various other outlets including Specsavers, Alliance and Leicester and the Hug website.

To get a quiz pack with everything you'll need from questions to balloons or for more information please visit www.allhug.org.uk or call 0870 770 3288.

Help the Aged is campaigning to improve services for isolated older people, and all money raised from the Hug campaign will continue to provide Help the Aged support services that allow older people to continue living independently and help them feel less alone.

This includes SeniorLink, which is the charity's 24-hour telephone service for use in emergencies and for a chat when needed, and the community transport scheme, Senior Mobility, to get older people to community centres to meet friends and engage in activities.

In addition, SeniorLine is the charity's telephone help and advice service on benefits take-up to enable people to have the money to participate more.

* Response from older people who regularly feel lonely

- The above information is from Help the Aged – see page 41 for their contact details.

© Help the Aged

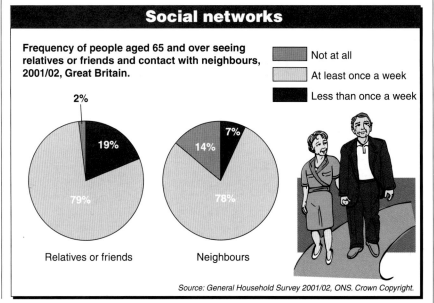

Social networks

Frequency of people aged 65 and over seeing relatives or friends and contact with neighbours, 2001/02, Great Britain.

Not at all
At least once a week
Less than once a week

Relatives or friends: 2%, 19%, 79%
Neighbours: 7%, 14%, 78%

Source: General Household Survey 2001/02, ONS. Crown Copyright.

Older people at risk of abuse

Information from Counsel and Care

What is abuse?

Abuse is behaviour towards other people which causes them any sort of harm or which puts them in danger, and includes being a victim of crime such as robbery, burglary and mugging. It can also occur in relationships where there is an expectation of trust or care.

Abuse of older people generally happens within a relationship. It is a single or repeated act or lack of appropriate action that is done to the older person by someone such as a relative, carer, neighbour or a member of staff at a care home or day centre. It is often also against the law but, because of the relationship that exists between the older person and the abuser, it can often feel difficult to report the abuse or stop it happening.

Older people can become the victims of crime, as they are often seen as an easy target. If you are a victim you should report the crime to the police. An organisation called Victim Support should contact you shortly after you have reported the crime to offer you advice and ensure you are well cared for. They can support you through any subsequent court action. Victim Support can also provide assistance to people who have been subject to a crime which has not been reported to the police.

Types of abuse

Abuse might occur in any of the following ways. Someone may be subjected to more than one form of abuse.

Abuse of older people generally happens within a relationship. It is a single or repeated act or lack of appropriate action that is done to the older person

---

Physical abuse

Physical abuse is most clearly identified in cases where there are signs of harm such as bruises, burns, broken skin or broken bones. However, there are less obvious types of physical abuse, for example, giving someone too much medication to make them drowsy and easier to look after or restraining someone by tying them to a chair or bed, or using furniture to stop them moving.

Psychological abuse

It is abusive to intimidate an older person by shouting, frightening, swearing at or ridiculing them. Other, more subtle forms of abuse might include blaming an older person for actions or behaviour that they are not able to control or trying to make them feel humiliated, rejected or ignored.

Financial abuse

Financial abuse includes illegal or improper use of a person's property, money, pension book, bank account or other valuables, as well as stealing money or property. If you are managing the finances of a person who does not have the mental capacity to do so for themselves, you should have an Enduring Power of Attorney or receivership to ensure that your actions are not mis-construed as financial abuse. An Enduring Power of Attorney is a legal document which authorises one or more people to handle another person's financial affairs, provided that it is registered with the Public Guardianship Office. (For more information, see factsheet 9: *Memory Loss, Depression, 'Confusion' and Dementia.*)

Sexual abuse

It is abusive to force an older person into any sexual activity that they do not want, including talking about sex or looking at books and videos.

Neglect

It is abusive to deprive a person of food, clothes, warmth and hygiene needs. Older people also have the right to have the health care treatment or medication they need. They also should not be isolated from social interaction or left unattended for periods of time if that puts them at risk or causes them distress or anxiety.

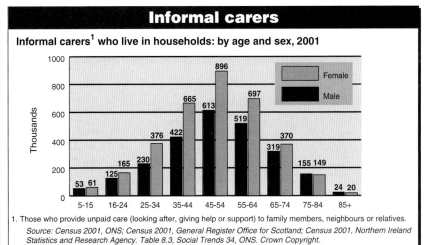

Informal carers

Informal carers[1] who live in households: by age and sex, 2001

1. Those who provide unpaid care (looking after, giving help or support) to family members, neighbours or relatives.

Source: Census 2001, ONS; Census 2001, General Register Office for Scotland; Census 2001, Northern Ireland Statistics and Research Agency. Table 8.3, Social Trends 34, ONS. Crown Copyright.

Symptoms of abuse

If an older person feels frightened and intimidated by being abused, they may not feel able to seek help. They may be unable to tell anyone about what is happening. They may need someone to take action on their behalf. The following may indicate someone is experiencing abuse:

- Recurring or unexplained injuries
- Untreated injuries and medical problems
- Frequent visits to the Accident and Emergency unit at hospital
- Being emotionally upset and agitated
- Inconsistency or difficulty in accounting for the cause of injuries
- The older person not being allowed to speak for themselves
- Poor personal hygiene, unchanged bedding and/or unsuitable clothing for the conditions or environment
- Untreated or long-standing pressure sores that are not healing
- Unexplained weight loss or gain, or evidence of dehydration noted by poor skin condition and/or frequent urine infections
- The older person appearing withdrawn, depressed, having irregular sleep patterns, low self-esteem, fearfulness, agitation, or loss of appetite
- Abrupt or unexplainable changes to bank accounts or wills.

Where does abuse occur?

Abuse can happen anywhere, but is most likely to occur in:

- The person's own home
- Hospital

- A care home
- Day centre or other social care centre.

It is often difficult for authorities to intervene if abuse is suspected or even if they know the older person is being abused

Who commits abuse?

Anyone may be an abuser, but according to statistics the following people are most likely to be in a position to mistreat an older person:

- 44% of abusers are family relatives
- 28% are paid carers
- 11% are friends and neighbours
- 2% are unpaid carers (a family member)
- 15% are in none of these categories.

Statistics provided by: Action on Elder Abuse, February 2005.

Who are the victims?

- The largest group, making up 22% of all people abused, are aged between 80 to 84
- Over half of all elder abuse is carried out on people aged 70 and over
- 67% are women, 22% are men and 11% are couples (the victim has a partner but they are still abused).

Difficulties in dealing with the abuse of older people

As with the abuse of any vulnerable person, there may be difficulties involved in the identification and resolution of the circumstances in which it occurs.

Identification of abuse may be difficult because the older person may feel embarrassed that they have 'allowed' it to happen. Preventing or stopping the abuse may be complicated because the older person may feel reluctant to make a complaint against the abuser. This could be through fear of the abuser or because the older person still has a meaningful relationship with the abuser. They may feel that they will not be believed. It may be that they do not recognise they are being abused.

A victim of abuse may feel traumatised by their experiences. These feelings may lead to a sense of low self-esteem with the older person quietly accepting the abuse.

An older person is an adult and therefore has the right to take risks and make their own decisions. This means that it is often difficult for authorities to intervene if abuse is suspected or even if they know that the older person is being abused, but does not want to do anything about it.

It is difficult to know what effect the different types of abuse will have on a person. The effects are likely to differ depending on whether it is a one-off instance of abuse or a continued series of abusive acts, or if the person relies on the abuser to meet their care needs.

- The above information is an extract from a Counsel and Care factsheet reprinted with permission. Visit www.counselandcare.org.uk

Older people in care homes

Feeling 'at home' enhances quality of life

Many frail, older people living in care homes are not being given the chance to be, quite simply, themselves, says research funded by the Economic and Social Research Council (ESRC). The research has broken new ground in getting perspectives from people living in care homes, including many with dementia and/or communication difficulties.

The project identified that 'being oneself', and feeling positive about it, enabled older people who can no longer live at home to enjoy a better quality of life. Government guidance is that carers should listen more to people in homes as a step towards improving their quality of life. But the researchers found that carers mostly have 'limited opportunities' to implement this guidance.

> *'Being oneself' . . . enabled older people who can no longer live at home to enjoy a better quality of life*

'People need to be able to express themselves', says Susan Tester, lead researcher. 'Their quality of life is inhibited if they are not able to feel "at home" and comfortable in expressing a sense of self positively.' Paying attention to how they look, valuing their possessions, showing that they like to have some personal space, all add to how they see themselves.

This sense of one's self is important in the relationships that people sustain with other residents in the home and with their families. Some manage to have contact with other residents even when their speech is impaired and their hearing poor. But some residents were hostile to others.

E·S·R·C ECONOMIC & SOCIAL RESEARCH COUNCIL

Trips outside the care home are rare and this confinement increases the risk of being cut off from past associations with neighbours and friends and family. Ordinary activities, like window shopping or going for a pint, were no longer possible. The quality of life of residents is determined almost wholly within the home. Relations with family, however, are important, particularly for the few in care who could keep up with their relatives and feel that they were still a part of the family. People with dementia, meanwhile, seemed to draw comfort in their relationships with family now dead.

The degree of control that people enjoyed in daily living was found to depend on the environment in which they lived and the sort of care they received as well as their own physical and mental aptitudes. The care staff had a key role in supporting people to help themselves. This was most notable in helping older people to be continent. Where people did not get this help, there was anger and distress on their part. Carers could also help enhance the quality of life by fostering caring personal relationships with residents. Likewise, they could inhibit it through lack of personal care and respect.

The research included focus groups, observations, carried out in four care home settings, guided conversations and individual observation of a sample of 52 residents from seven care homes. The participants included 41 women and 11 men, in age groups from 65-69 to 95-99, the majority in the 75-89 range. 24 had been diagnosed with dementia. Conversation methods included the use of Talking Mats, a visual framework using picture symbols to help people with communication difficulties.

■ The above information is from the Economic and Social Research Council – visit www.esrc.ac.uk or see page 41 for address details.

© ESRC

Age – a relevant value?

Information from Communigate

'You're as young as you feel'
'Age is just a number'
'You look young for your age'
'Young at heart'

Statements used as ways of coping with society's general non-acceptance of the older person. More often than not, older women are treated as less acceptable or desirable than older men.

There are times when younger people are subjected to ageism. If someone is considered old enough to vote at eighteen then they are old enough to be taken seriously.

There is no disputing that someone will experience ageism at some point in their life just as there is no disputing that it is females that are most likely to experience this prejudicial treatment.

You only have to look in the 'lonely hearts' sections of publications to see ageism at work. A forty-something woman on the one hand, advertising her age, e.g 'bubbly lady, 43 seeking soulmate', is expected to be grateful for the opportunity to date a string of fifty-plus or even sixty-plus gentlemen (some of whom may be very nice incidentally). Generally, she would not be seen as a suitable companion for a 20 to 35-year-old man.

On the other hand, a 43-year-old man could go out with a 25-year-old woman and no one would bat an eyelid, whereas, a younger man would generally think he could 'do better' than an older woman. His mum would disapprove and his friends make jokes about him going out with someone 'old enough to be his mum'. If someone implies that you're 'too old' to date, look for someone younger still to take you out! Even if it's only once your self-esteem will be restored.

Employers are keen to state the requirement for 'youthful' individuals when advertising a vacancy. How rude these advertisements are, cleverly discouraging anyone over 30 years of age from applying without there being any blatant discrimination for which a firm may be punished. Are older women only good enough to advertise anti-ageing creams?

It's as if everyone becomes useless on hitting 30. If you've not made it before then, plenty will make sure you don't afterwards. An individual experiences depreciation in value, their worth in society becoming less and less as years go by. Better not tell the Prime Minister and his wife then!

But how many twentysomethings are running the country? I rest my case.

Though is it a matter of experience only counting in certain places? In contrast, if experience counted everywhere, everyone under 30 would suffer ageism so the problem would still be in existence.

The key is striking a balance, with every individual to be afforded the same amount of respect as any other individual. Whether or not this can be achieved lies within the mind of every individual.

If you feel you have experienced ageism then we suggest that you write to your local councillor or MP. If businesses will not employ you due to genuine age prejudice, write to their HQ and complain. At the very least you will feel better.

A person has a lot more to offer than how old they are. Everyone has unique qualities irrespective of their age. Age prejudice is cruel and unjust – do not accept it.

■ The above information is from the This Is Bradford website at www.thisisbradford.co.uk

© Communigate

Ageism

Ageism, or discriminating against people purely on the grounds of their chronological age, is deeply embedded and very widespread in our society

Age discrimination is very often unconscious which makes it difficult to tackle. People sometimes think they are being kind if they treat older people differently from those who are younger.

Their attitude will be felt as patronising and will harm the self-esteem of the individual and demean society as a whole.

The main reason for eradicating this harmful behaviour is that our society is undergoing a huge demographic revolution.

In future we will need to utilise the skills, experience and energy of healthier, more active and dynamic older generations. A multi-generational workforce will ensure our economy will prosper in a highly competitive world.

Ageing 'a triumph'

The ageing of the population is an unprecedented triumph resulting from the huge advances in medical and social care, but the challenges it presents to us can also be seen as daunting.

It impacts on many areas of life, from the design of our homes and workplaces, which need to be inclusive, to access to education and training opportunities, which need to be genuinely lifelong.

Some of us can learn or acquire skills and education better when we are more mature and the ever changing nature of work will require people of all ages to update their knowledge.

Currently arbitrary age barriers mean older citizens can't participate in many voluntary and civic activities, such as being a magistrate after a particular birthday.

As consumers older people may have difficulty hiring a car, getting insurance or borrowing money just because they have reached a certain age.

Health discrimination

In healthcare, the discrimination is evident when older patients in the NHS are treated differently from the young.

Examples include omitting older people from clinical trials or denying particular treatment or operations on the basis of their chronological age.

Health and longevity can equate to a greater national wealth because healthy older individuals can remain productive members of society for longer

---

Such decisions are unjustified and arbitrary, based on prejudiced views of what a 'good innings' is or that the interventions are not worth pursuing because a person is 'old'.

On the contrary, these older people often respond better because they are by definition 'survivors' and might make a more successful recovery than a less hardy younger person.

As older people are major consumers of medicine their exclusion from clinical trials makes little medical sense.

Old are taxpayers too

As our society ages, it's important that good health continues into later life.

Health and longevity can equate to a greater national wealth because healthy older individuals can remain productive members of society for longer, consuming goods and services and contributing as workers, and therefore taxpayers, and also as volunteers who are the mainstay of civil society.

For employers, enforcing arbitrary retirement ages instead of using a real appraisal of a person's competence ignores the fact that some people are ineffective at 75 and others at 35.

Many people today are innovative and achieving new goals well into their 80s and beyond.

We are all different and the number of our birthdays is not the best indicator of how we differ.

Age discrimination is a huge waste of talent. There is legislation due to come into effect in October 2006 banning age discrimination in employment and training.

The impending establishment of a Commission for Equality and Human Rights will have a role to promote age equality and will look to develop inclusive patterns of employment for all areas of diversity.

Entrenched attitudes take a long time to change.

In employment it may be difficult for a young manager to tell an older colleague that they must change their way of working because their work no longer represents current best practice.

Performance management throughout a person's career is therefore essential so we can benefit from a person's experience regardless of age, and work towards the age diverse workforce we need, where youth and experience combine to give us the strengths the global economy requires.

Pushing the frontiers

Today's older people have lived through more change than any preceding generations.

They are the ones who developed today's computer technology and space travel, broke the genetic code and pushed the frontiers of science forward.

People like Bill Gates and indeed Mick Jagger are no longer young but should not be put in a box marked 'past their sell by date'.

Apart from anything else those now aged 50+ won't tolerate being thrown on the scrap heap. They have a huge amount of offer to society.

That's why politicians will have to listen to what they want.

Not only are their numbers increasing but they are the people most likely to vote in elections.

■ The above information is from the Seniors Network and is reprinted with permission – visit their website at www.seniorsnetwork.co.uk
© Seniors Network 2004

Legislation on age discrimination

Information from the University of Westminster

Although there is no legislation at present on age discrimination in employment in the UK the UK Government has committed to the EU Directive to introduce age discrimination legislation by December 2006. In 1999, however, the Government introduced a Code of Practice on Age Diversity in Employment.

What is the Code of Practice on Age Diversity in Employment?

This is a voluntary set of good practice standards to help employers recognise the business benefits of an age-diverse workforce. The Code encourages employers to make decisions that do not discriminate on the basis of age.

What does the Code cover?

The Code covers the following six aspects of the employment cycle:
■ Recruitment: based on the skills and abilities needed to do the job.
■ Selection: based on merit focusing on the application form, information about skills and abilities and on performance at interview.
■ Promotion: based on the ability, or demonstrated potential, to do the job.
■ Training and Development: all employees should be encouraged to take advantage of relevant training opportunities.
■ Redundancy: based on objective, job-related criteria to ensure the skills needed to help the business are retained.
■ Retirement: retirement schemes should be applied fairly taking both individual and business needs into account.

Has the Code made any difference?

Interim evaluation of the Code has indicated that:
■ A third of employers are now aware of the Code.
■ Use of age specification in recruitment has halved since July 1999.
■ 75% of new equal opportunities policies now include reference to age.

The Code is voluntary. Are there any plans to make age discrimination in employment illegal?

In November 2000 the UK Government committed to the EU Employment Directive (Article 13) which means it must introduce age discrimination legislation by December 2006. This means that the UK will have fully comprehensive age discrimination legislation for the first time. This legislation will have the same weight as legislation on gender, race and disability.

As a first step towards such legislation the UK Government has formed an Age Advisory Group which is presently conducting an in-depth consultation process to gain the views of employers, older workers and younger workers.

■ The above information is from the University of Westminster website which can be found at www.wmin.ac.uk

© University of Westminster

Flexible working in an ageing society

Issues for the older workforce – and the rest of us

Outlawing age discrimination and introducing policies for flexible retirement are goals of the UK government. According to Minister of State for Pensions Malcolm Wicks:

'There are too many men and women in their 50s and early 60s who would like another job, but because of age discrimination find it almost impossible to get one. There's something ridiculous about being told at 53 or 54 that you are too old when you have another 30 years of life ahead.

'That kind of ageism can be as debilitating and cruel to the individual as being told you can't have a job because you are black or because you have a disability. This kind of discrimination is going to be outlawed in 2006.

'We are making progress, but too many people are out of work in that pre-retirement period.

Currently around one-third of people between the ages of 50 and state pension age are not working

---

'There is an anchor question here, about the retirement age at work – not when you can get the state pension. That is, whether we should be much more liberal about when we are expected to retire. We need to move to a situation where there is far more flexibility about people making choices about when they work and when they retire – in their 60s or maybe later.'

(Speech at Future East conference in late 2004).

Too many people are indeed 'out of work in the pre-retirement period'. And the cost to companies and the UK economy is high.

According to a report, *The Economic Contribution of Older People*, published by Age Concern, GDP is from £12 billion up to £30 billion lower than it might be otherwise because of the underemployment of older people.

An ageing population

The underemployment of older workers is happening at a time when society as a whole is ageing:

- average life expectancy now is 76 for men and 80 for women
- by 2050 this is expected to be over 80 for men and over 85 for women
- by 2021 there will be more people over 80 than there are children under 5
- In twenty years time there will be two million fewer adults aged between 16 and 50 and two million more between 50 and state pension age.

It has been said that we are now moving from a 3-generation to a 4-generation society. That is, one where it is becoming normal rather than the exception for 4 generations of the same family to be alive at the same time. People in their 60s and 70s are increasingly depended on by elderly parents, rather than being themselves at the top of the generational tree.

Couple this with a pensions crisis where many people now under 60 will not have enough income after retirement, there is an overwhelming economic need for people to rethink what retirement means for them.

Is working for ever what I want?

The implication of this is that people need to work longer, and postpone retirement.

At the same time, few people want to work flat out beyond the current retirement age. In fact, workplace surveys usually show that older staff are very actively thinking about working differently – either scaling down their work, working different hours, or spending one or two days per week working from home.

There has also been an increasing trend, often profiled in the weekend supplements, to downshifting – stepping out of the rat race to do what you really want to do, though it means earning less money. It may mean cashing in on a valuable property and moving to somewhere where property prices are cheaper, and leading a more simple – but more fulfilled – life.

In many ways new technologies make this option more possible. Contacts both with markets and family can be maintained over greater distances.

What are older workers doing now?

Currently around one-third of people between the ages of 50 and state pension age are not working.

Within this age group, one can expect employment rates to be somewhat lower due to people taking early retirement and due to acquired disability or long-term illness. However, this does not account for the extent of economic inactivity.

Nor should we make easy assumptions that people who have retired and people with disabilities do not want to do any work, and effectively exclude them from the labour market.

Older people are more likely to be doing part-time or temporary work than any other age group, apart from the youngest age group (16-24) of students and school and college leavers.

A clear majority (77% of men and 91% of women) indicate that they are working part-time out of preference rather than because they cannot get a full-time job.

So there is demand for part-time working. But in most forms of employment, it is hard to make the transition to part-time work from a full-time post.

Older workers are also more likely than other age groups to be self-employed. This may in part be explained statistically by the number of employees in this age group who take early retirement, but it does not explain the whole picture.

What it shows is that many older people are using their skills and experience to run their own enterprises. But recent research shows that lenders are usually reluctant to invest in new ventures started by the over-50s.

What will the new legislation do?

The new age discrimination legislation is the UK's response to a European Directive on Equal Treatment in Employment.

The government has made it clear that legislation to ban age discrimination will take effect from October 2006, although it is not yet entirely clear how exactly it will work.

However, following an extensive consultation process and a recent decision about the future retirement age, it seems likely that the legislation will:

- ban any discriminatory procedures in recruitment on the grounds of age – this includes workers at any age, not only older workers
- outlaw age-related harassment in the workplace on the lines of current gender equality legislation

---

> *Older people are more likely to be doing part-time or temporary work than any other age group, apart from the youngest age group (16-24) of students and school and college leavers*

- outlaw workplace benefits that are age-related (which could be bad news for some older workers)
- set a default retirement age of 65 – so outlawing arbitrary earlier retirement ages, and also giving the worker at 65 the 'right to request' to continue working beyond this age. As with the recent parental flexible working rights, the employer is obliged to consider this request.

But there is no right to request flexible working associated – just a right to request continuing to work.

These provisions are thought not to go far enough by campaigners, but are thought to be potentially very costly by employers' organisations. Due to the loose ends lawyers are outwardly furrowing brows, while inwardly beaming with delight at a potential new income stream.

Flexibility says...

It's a first step. Effectively it will introduce a flexible retirement age. But this does not mean that employers will address flexible retirement issues.

Some barriers are being removed, but it will take more than this legislation to encourage discouraged older workers to re-enter the workforce, and to make people approaching retirement want to continue working.

Greater flexibility in working arrangements should be part of the equation, but that is also not the whole answer. Pensions provision needs also to move into a new era of flexible retirement, so that workers know they will not be penalised in any way for continuing to work or by adopting flexible working practices towards the end of their working lives.

But in any area of life, governments will only do so much. Employers can take the lead in making themselves the 'employer of choice' for older workers, by enabling working patterns that meet the needs of this section of the labour market.

- The above information is used with permission of Flexibility, the online journal of flexible work – visit www.flexibility.co.uk for more.

© *Flexibility*

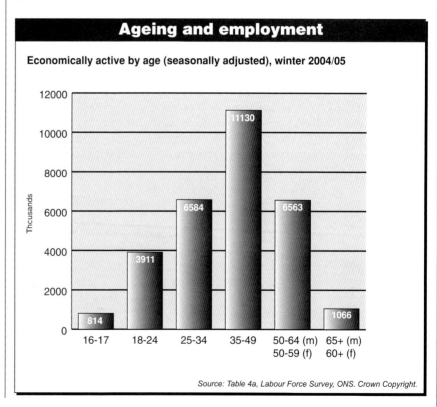

Ageing and employment

Economically active by age (seasonally adjusted), winter 2004/05

Source: Table 4a, Labour Force Survey, ONS. Crown Copyright.

Discrimination against older women

Information from Liverpool John Moores University

Ageism is widely recognised as a prime area of discrimination at work, but do older women face greater disadvantage because of their gender and their ageing? A new study by Liverpool John Moores University reports on the hidden dimension of ageism in paid employment.

The government has promised to make it illegal to discriminate in employment on the grounds of age. Although UK legislation is required by December 2006, there is much debate about what form it should take: Should it include a gender dimension? Should it focus on all age groups or older workers in particular? Most of all, will a legislative approach prove effective in combating the more subtle and disguised forms of age prejudice? A new research project by Liverpool John Moores University, with funding from the European Social Fund (ESF), invites men and women aged 50 and over to contribute to this debate.

Over the past two decades there has been a dramatic decline in the employment of older people, while overall employment rates have continued to rise. According to figures published by Age Concern, there are over 2 million people aged 50-65 currently out of work. The under-representation of this age group is most often explained as an outcome of age prejudice based on culturally prevalent images of older people in general. The recurrent theme is that older workers are thought to be: past their work prime, less productive, more expensive and difficult to manage. There is also evidence of 'early exit' with increasing numbers of older men leaving work before state retirement age due to a range of factors including ill health and redundancy. Although the participation rates for older women have risen in recent years to 67% in 2003, the majority of women over 50 are concentrated in low paid, low status and part-time work.

Despite nearly 30 years of Equal Opportunity Legislation, women continue to remain at a relative disadvantage, particularly with respect to training, promotion and general treatment at work. The Equal Pay Task Force also found that women in full-time work earn just 82p for every £1 earned by men. In addition, the time spent outside the labour market to have and raise children has meant that women are often forced to play catch-up to the male model of career progression. It is argued that women generally face a 40-plus barrier to promotion – some ten years earlier than men in equivalent occupations.

As part of a much larger research project funded by the European Social Fund (ESF), 12 women aged 50 and over were invited to share their experiences of age-related matters in paid employment. We wanted to know if they had encountered ageism (past and present) and if so how did their experience(s) impact on their conditions of employment? How did it affect their ability to take control of their career progression? How did it impact upon their relationships with co-workers? The women were from a variety of employment sectors.

Seven of the 12 women interviewed said that they had encountered discrimination in early adulthood based on their gender, their ageing or a combination of these factors. Most of the women had confronted classic gendered assumptions about motherhood, the care of the family and their role within it. It was felt that employers at that time (1960s, early 1970s) thought women were only interested in work until they got married or had children:

'Back then men thought you couldn't do this and you couldn't do that or you were just keeping this job until you became pregnant and started a family and then you'd go part time or stay at home, but you wouldn't have a career.'

Looking back on their time in employment, most of the women felt that what they had seen and experienced in their past was of relevance to the ways in which they (as older women) were now experiencing and dealing with gender-ageist messages:

'I am more determined for it not to bother me and so I make an extra effort, and it's the same effort I made in the 70s when I came up against prejudice because I was female. It is the same prejudice now except they're looking at me now thinking, "Aged 50 will be slow to learn".'

But for other women the accumulation of negative treatment at various points in their life course had a profound effect on their self-esteem and often determined whether they felt willing or able to take on new opportunities at work:

'When you're fifty, you've had a few people say "no" to you and so that draws you back. I don't know if it is because of my age or the way I've been treated in the past that I don't have the confidence to take on new challenges. I feel as if I've had the stuffing knocked out of me.'

In addition, some of the women in jobs that were stressful and/or demanding reported confrontation with ageist stereotypes about mental decline and intellectual capacity:

'Because I'm older they (co-workers) naturally assume that it will take me longer.'

Nearly all of the women interviewed mentioned the gendered nature of ageing in paid employment, particularly in respect to a double standard:

'Very few women in their 50s are as successful as men in their 50s... only the odd one.'

It was also felt that women are valued in accordance to the conditions ascribed to youth (energy, image) whereas men are valued in accordance to their (older) age and maturity.

This study examined the gender dimension of ageism from the perspective of a diverse group of older women. It illustrated the extent to which gender discrimination and ageist perceptions combined and interacted to limit the potential of women in organisations. The women interviewed reported confrontation with ageist discourse about intellectual decline and age-appropriate behaviour and felt that these had occurred in isolation or in combination with gender discourse about image/youthfulness and the 'proper place' for *older* women.

The general conclusion drawn is that gender or ageing alone, or the primacy of one over the other, will provide little insight into the kind of discrimination facing women in their 50s. The results of this aspect of the research appear to support the existence of a 'double jeopardy' or 'double burden' of gender-age discrimination. This finding has significant policy implications, particularly in relation to forthcoming legislation on age discrimination.

■ This information was written by Dr Diane Grant, Dr Mark Meadows and Helen Walker and is reprinted with permission from Liverpool John Moores University – view the text at http://livjm.ac.uk/olf/gdap.

90 *not out*

Teenager to old timer, the worker who never wants to retire

He retired once before and didn't like it.

So at 90, Sidney Prior is determined to keep working as long as he can.

The man who started his career as a 14-year-old office boy is enjoying every moment of his job as a gardening assistant at B&Q.

He gets up at 4am every day, cooks himself a full English breakfast and prepares a packed lunch before catching the Tube to work.

'I just like working,' he said as he celebrated his birthday with colleagues and customers at the store in Wimbledon, South-West London.

Mr Prior, who was born in Horsham, Sussex, started work 76 years ago in a company providing tools for the engineering trade.

'Things were very different then,' he said. 'The first time I heard the wireless was in 1924. We all had to wear trilbys and raise our hats whenever we saw a lady. I was earning 10 shillings a week, about 50p.'

When war broke out he became a sergeant in the Royal Corps of Signals laying communication lines to frontline troops in North Africa and Italy.

After the war he returned to work as a salesman, but decided on a change. 'I wanted to do something different so I joined a company importing machine tools.'

Over the next 25 years he enjoyed a lucrative sales career, travelling all over Europe. But company policy demanded retirement at 65 and he had to leave.

'I didn't like it at all. I had nothing to do, I didn't just want to sit at home,' he recalled.

Three months later he was back at work, helping his nephew in a grocery firm. Ten years later, when the nephew moved abroad, he found himself at a loose end again.

'I was suddenly sitting at home at 76 in an upstairs flat and I thought "this is not for me",' he said. So he joined B&Q, which has a policy of employing older workers.

'There are lots of people who come here and say, "when are you going to retire, Sid?" and I say "Never I hope, unless I am forced to or when they shoot me".'

He works a 31-hour week at the store and earns £7,500, plus three bonuses a year and five weeks' paid holiday.

Mr Prior, from Fulham, said meeting people was one of the perks of the job. And he enjoys the camaraderie of his colleagues.

'Working with people of all ages gives youngsters the chance to learn a little from an old timer like myself, and they help to keep me young at heart,' he said.

Nearly a quarter of B&Q's 37,000 staff are over 50. Its oldest employee is 91-year-old Reg Hill, who works at the Swindon branch in Wiltshire.

Chief Executive Rob Cissell visited the Wimbledon store yesterday in honour of Mr Prior's birthday.

'He is the epitome of someone who we think should be able to work if he wants or needs to,' he said. 'With his positive attitude and his energy he's a real bonus to the business.'

Why sixty is the new forté

What's the best age to be working? Recent research may persuade employers to rethink the concept of careers – and to stop cherry-picking workers from a particular age group

By Katie Hope

The older you are, the happier you are at work, according to research published yesterday (23 February 2005). And it reveals that people in their sixties enjoy work more than any other age group. While a cynic may say their optimism comes from them nearing the end of their working lives, the research reveals that almost one in five is dreading retirement. This age group is also happier to work until they are 70 than any other.

And that, says Sam Mercer, director of the Employers' Forum on Age, which commissioned the research, is the point. 'We wanted to overturn the stereotypes,' she says. 'The research provides a source of reliable and robust data so government and employers can make policy decisions based on clear and understandable research rather than relying on stereotypes.'

People in their sixties enjoy work more than any other age group

The *Age at Work* guide is based on 1,636 interviews with a cross-section of the working population, coupled with analysis of the 2003/04 Office for National Statistics' Labour Force Survey.

Split into six age groups – teens, twenties, thirties, forties, fifties and sixties – the study aims to help employers better understand the impact of age on workforce behaviour and attitudes.

The findings suggest people of all ages are held back by an outdated idea of careers, where the young start at the bottom and retirement is a cliff edge at the peak. In particular, it reveals the frustration of employees in their teens and twenties. Only a quarter say they are regularly given an interesting challenge, with 21 per cent claiming their work is 'boring'. This is in contrast to those in their sixties, who are more confident and happy to work than is typically believed, with 93 per cent saying they like their jobs.

'The perceived wisdom is that you start out great and get worse but work isn't so great at the start, and it gets better,' says Mercer. She adds that the results show employers the necessity of investment and training throughout people's working lives.

'Employers must look at how better to harness the energy and enthusiasm of employees, including those in their sixties, because they are clearly not just marking time until retirement,' says Mercer.

However, another key finding is that people in more physically demanding work find it harder as they get older, with 43 per cent of people in their fifties in skilled manual labour saying their age affected performance. This decreases to 16 per cent for people in professional roles.

Mercer says this shows employers need to help ease the transition into a second career for such people, and this needs to begin in people's forties. But 27 per cent of people in that age group feel stuck in a rut, rising to 48 per cent for people in their sixties. They feel they have no choice but to stay in their current situations.

A third (31 per cent) of those in their forties also do not feel they will achieve their goals in life, the lowest of any generation. 'It's important we don't underestimate how big a shift needs to take place. It is so deeply entrenched in the cultural psyche that you start at the bottom and work your way up that the idea of starting again in your forties is not culturally acceptable,' says Mercer.

Yet, by 2006, 45- to 59-year-olds will form the largest group in the workforce and life expectancy is increasing by one year every four years. In 2006, for the first time, there will be more 55- to 64-year-olds than 16- to 24-year-olds in the UK.

'We are storing up problems for the future,' Mercer warns. 'Employers shouldn't cherry-pick specific ages. It is about investing in people in the long term rather than choosing the easiest option.'

To respond, Mercer says diversity functions within HR should, in the process of bringing in policies, examine the barriers to work that exclude different types of people.

'Many employers have great policies but their practices do not reflect this. Looking at all HR policies with a mind to diversity helps companies to identify issues: the fact that you are not retaining young people, or that women tend to leave in their mid-thirties, for example,' says Mercer.

The research shows age directly links with sex, with women more likely than men to have been put off applying for a job because of age. It also shows that from their teens, more men than women reach management positions.

From 1 October 2006 it will be illegal to discriminate on the basis of age. Mercer believes age legislation could strengthen sexual discrimination claims.

By 2006, 45- to 59-year-olds will form the largest group in the workforce

'In Ireland, where there is age legislation, sex has been an issue. For example, an employer calling someone "a young foolish girl" makes it a double-discrimination claim, whereas gender on its own may not stand up,' says Mercer.

Although the government has yet to publish final details of the age legislation, Mercer says the research makes it clear employers need to start preparing now. 'The message coming through clearly from this research is how angry and frustrated many employees are. They are beginning to articulate this and they will bring claims,' says Mercer.

The second part of *Age at Work*, which analyses how factors other than age influence employees' expectations of work, will be published in September. For more details see www.efa.org.uk

Age at work: key findings

- Teens – 25 per cent of teenagers have been put off applying for a job because of their age, the highest of any generation.
- Twenties – 37 per cent of men and 24 per cent of women in this age group have already reached management positions. Here, the management gap between the sexes is at its narrowest.
- Thirties – Only 54 per cent of people are happy with the balance between their work and leisure time, which is the lowest of any generation.
- Forties – 26 per cent of people in this age group who are leaving their previous job cite health as the reason, although evidence suggests they move to other types of jobs rather than becoming economically inactive.
- Fifties – 74 per cent of people say they like to keep up with new technology, a mere 5 per cent lower than those in their teens.
- Sixties – 93 per cent of respondents say they like their work, the highest of any age group.

Younger workers

'The two greatest issues we face with people in their twenties is attracting them, then retaining them, and that is clear from this research,' says Sarah Churchman, head of student recruitment and diversity at PricewaterhouseCoopers.

The research shows 70 per cent of people in that age group, the highest after teens, believe having a clear career path is important.

Churchman says PricewaterhouseCoopers addresses this by making clear to people the options available within and outside the company, including going into industry or transferring overseas on the basis that people may choose to rejoin the company after these experiences.

The research also shows that the number of people in their twenties resigning is second only to teenagers, suggesting a willingness to change jobs to improve income.

'Many people join us on a graduate training scheme and don't always know they could double or, in some cases, treble their current package within three years, so we make it clear what is on offer to them,' Churchman says.

- The above information was originally published in *People Management* magazine on 24/2/05 and is reproduced with permission of CIPD. For their contact details see page 41.
© CIPD

Age discrimination hits young people too

Information from Age Positive

The talents of workers are being wasted by companies who judge them by how old they are, rather than their contribution to the business, warns a new study by the Employers' Forum on Age (EFA).

Sam Mercer, Director of the EFA, says: 'We need to break the stereotype habit. Employers must recognise that a "one size fits all" approach is flawed. It would make much more sense to find ways to retain and motivate workers, and offer flexibility, training and development – irrespective of age.'

It's a myth that age discrimination only affects the 50+ age group – reveals EFA's *Age at Work* study. Ageism at work appears to be a bigger problem for people in their late teens than their 50s.

- 25% of school leavers have faced age discrimination compared to 21% of those over 50 and 18% of those over 60.
- Young people are denied interesting and challenging jobs, which is why they move on frequently: it's nothing to do with a lack of loyalty.
- 70% of those in their 20s believe a career path is important – the highest among all groups, yet only 25% are given interesting challenges and 21% claim what they do is boring.
- People in their 50s and 60s aren't all rushing to retire: 30% of people are happy to work until they're 70 and 13% dread retirement, a feeling that increases with age.
- People are happier at work the older they get: 93% of the over 60s like work – the highest among all age groups.

- The above information is from Age Positive's website which can be found at www.agepositive.gov.uk, or see page 41 for their address details.
© Crown Copyright

What is the pensions crisis?

Information from Help the Aged

We constantly read stories in the media about our ageing population and the consequent pensions crisis.

The 'crisis' has been caused by a combination of longer life expectancy and falling stock market returns. This has resulted in there not being enough money stored in pension funds to guarantee a comfortable retirement for people who are currently at work.

The UK population is set to increase gradually from 59.2 million in 2002 to 64.8 million by 2031. The average (mean) age of the population is also set to rise from 39.3 in 2002 to 43.6 by 2031. The number of people over retirement age is projected to rise by 11.9 per cent, from 10.9 million in 2002 to 12.2 million in 2011. Simply put, we live in a country which will have more older people who will live for longer.

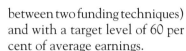

The way forward
Help the Aged believes that the way forward out of the pensions crisis is as follows:

- People should be entitled to expect a decent income in retirement, funded both by tax/National Insurance and investment products (so spreading risk between two funding techniques) and with a target level of 60 per cent of average earnings.
- There must be a solid and dependable triangular relationship between government, the employer and the working citizen in which both rights and responsibilities are clearly communicated, understood and upheld.
- An independent pension authority should exist to supervise this relationship and remove it from the 'short termism' of the political environment.
- All working citizens should expect to pay more for decent pensions and should be compelled to do so on an income-related scale. Employers must contribute too.
- Social security benefits should be reserved for small groups with special needs. The mainstream should not need this support.
- More working (and contributing) years will be necessary in an ageing society but this should be achieved by choice. The concept of fixed retirement and pension ages must be examined.
- Age discrimination must be vigorously attacked, not least in the workplace, and, in setting working patterns and retraining employment practices, must be transformed, to encourage older workers.

What is pensioner poverty?
The UK is the world's fourth richest country yet more than two million pensioners live below the poverty line. The older you are the greater your chances of living in poverty and this lack of income can have even wider-ranging effects – with poverty closely linked to ill health, disability and lower life expectancy.

Increase the State Pension to a 'decency' level
The basic State Pension (SP) is £79.60 for a single person and £127.25 for a couple. Help the Aged believes that the SP should be set at the minimum 'decency' level necessary to meet essential needs.

Research from the Family Budget Unit into income needs has shown that to pay for the basic requirements of a healthy, palatable diet, adequate heating and transport, a single pensioner requires an income of £99-£125 a week.

The number of people over retirement age is projected to rise by 11.9 per cent, from 10.9 million in 2002 to 12.2 million in 2011

Help the Aged believes that increasing the SP in line with earnings is the fairest and simplest way to lift pensioners out of poverty.

Pension Credit, the Government's flagship benefit for older people, goes some way towards addressing this but not far enough. The downside is that the new Credit is 'ferociously difficult to understand'.

The positives of Pension Credit are that it provides £2bn more for pensioners over 65 and Help the Aged will be encouraging as many older people as possible to claim the money to which they are entitled.

- The above information is from Help the Aged's website which can be found at www.helptheaged.org.uk, or see page 41 for contact details.

© Help the Aged

Money talk

An employment expert outlines the benefits of encouraging more older people back into the workforce

By Keith Frost, Spokesman

Barely a day seems to go by without a fresh warning that we will have to work longer and save more.

The UK, like most developed western countries, faces a demographic time bomb. The UK's ageing population means that in the not too distant future there will be too few workers to pay the pensions of older people.

Policymakers have woken to the fact that we need to have a greater number of middle-aged and older people employed. In fact, the UK's pension problems will not be solved unless we allow people to work longer.

After all, unless there are opportunities for people to continue working throughout their 50s and early 60s, then the vast majority have little chance of saving for their 70s and 80s and beyond.

But what seems to have been largely ignored is that the decision on whether to work up to state pension age, let alone beyond it, is frequently taken by someone other than the individuals themselves. Presently, workers over 50 are twice as likely to be made redundant as their colleagues in their 30s or 40s in any organisational restructuring or downsizing.

Recently, the National Audit Office (NAO) reported that: 'Of those who are early retired, no more than one-third chose to leave employment voluntarily.' Nearly 50% of those retiring early go straight onto welfare benefits and remain on them till they are old enough to draw the state pension. Given suitable support and opportunities, many could be contributing rather than depending.

Stereotypes

When asked, employers cite the following key reasons for why they don't employ older workers.
- Older workers are marking time until they can retire.
- They are less productive and don't want to learn new skills or techniques.
- Older workers take more time off, are in poorer health and cost more.

From October 2006 age discrimination will be outlawed unless it can be objectively justified

The evidence doesn't support these stereotypes.

The reality is that the majority of people have retirement thrust upon them either as the result of a temporary bout of ill-health, redundancy or because they have reached some arbitrary age. In the vast majority of modern jobs, older workers are not less productive. Given the opportunity, encouragement and right environment, many are happy and anxious to learn.

They are not marking time and want to work.

The NAO estimates that age discrimination in the workplace is costing the UK economy £31bn a year.

It is true that workers that have been with a company for many years can cost more in wages and pensions than an employee who has just joined. However, average gross hourly wage for those aged 50 to state pension age is over 8% below that for 25- to 49-year-olds. Likewise professional salaries can be on average 20% lower.

In addition, older workers take no more time off sick than their younger counterparts.

Outlawed

From October 2006 age discrimination will be outlawed unless it can be objectively justified by the employer. The regulations will apply to all people of working age – not just older workers.

The majority of employers have not begun to prepare for the regulations, nor considered the far-reaching changes they will need to make to their employment policies and practices. The regulations will provide a necessary backstop but in themselves are unlikely to lead to the cultural changes needed.

However, a host of UK employers have started to wake up to the benefits of having an age-diverse workforce. Asda, Barclays, B&Q, BT, HBOS, Marks & Spencer and Sainsbury's have all benefited from employing older workers.

These firms recognise that older workers bring a wealth of experience, actual and transferable skills, commitment, loyalty, good customer service skills and reliability.

And by getting more middle-aged and older people into work, perhaps the UK can diffuse the demographic time bomb.

- The above information is reprinted with kind permission from the Third Age Employment Network – for more information, visit their website at www.taen.org.uk

UK employers must retain 50+ workers

Retention of older workers is central to affordable pensions, says the Work Foundation

Responding to the Pensions Commission report published today, 12 October 2004, the Work Foundation called on employers, employers' bodies and the TUC to do far more to reverse the culture of early retirement and voluntary redundancy that has allowed too many over 50s to leave the labour market.

As the Pensions Commission have rightly pointed out, raising the participation rate of those in work and also getting those out of work back to work is a critical element in earning more to save more for longer retirements and preventing poverty in retirement. If the retirement age is to be raised to 67 or even 70 then employers will need to be encouraged to recruit and retain older staff.

As David Coats, Associate Director – Policy at the Work Foundation, says, 'The Pensions Commission report is clear and precise. UK workers need to save much more in order to afford their future retirement. This can be done by a combination of working longer, saving far more of our earnings while working, the State providing more pension contribution by raising taxes to pay for it and getting more people into work who are currently not working and so not saving or paying taxes.'

He continues, 'On the last point there are nearly 8 million economically inactive people of working age, including over 3.1 million men, on top of 1.4 million people actively seeking work of which 820,000 are men. Many of these people, particularly older men, have been made redundant or have lost their jobs because employers, and some groups of employees, believe that retiring at 50 plus helps ease pressure at the top of organisations and clears out the deadwood. Not only is this wrong, in most cases it is a policy at odds with the thrust of the Pensions Commission analysis. A policy of keeping people working won't work if employers insist on sticking to a sell-by date for their employees.'

Central to retaining older workers well into their 60s will be a more flexible approach from employers to those workers' employment terms and conditions. Home working, part-time working, the use of flexi-time, control over shift patterns are all part of the solution. Offering older workers longer breaks at different times of the year or sabbaticals can help keep valuable experience locked in.

As Mr Coats says, 'Time and task flexibility is particularly valuable for older workers. If we are all going to have to save more and work longer then we need to engage workers throughout their working lifecycle. This means employers valuing experience and understanding how best to utilise it across the organisation. It means enabling people to work smarter, not longer hours, and it means employers understanding that individuals should be judged on

their skills, ability and experience – not on whether they are young or old.'

It is also clear that we need to make it easier to help over 50s into self-employment. For older people create longer-lasting businesses. The accumulated knowledge, experience and easier access to finance means that the average 50-year-old setting up a business can expect that business to last twice as long as an average 20-year-old's business – 5 years instead of 2.5 years. Furthermore entrepreneurs over 55 are enjoying a business survival rate of 70% after 6 years compared with 19% average for all start-ups.

Entrepreneurs over 55 are enjoying a business survival rate of 70% after 6 years compared with 19% average for all start-ups

---

Mr Coats adds, 'The Pensions Commission has highlighted the crisis at the heart of our pensions system. There are no quick fixes. The arithmetic is simple. We must all work longer and save more. That means killing the early retirement culture and encouraging all employers to recognise the value that older workers can bring. It means redoubling our efforts to get people back to work who are currently economically inactive and it means fast-tracking more flexible forms of working to enable this to happen.'

■ The above information is from the Work Foundation's website at www.theworkfoundation.com, or see page 41 for contact details.

© The Work Foundation

Goodbye geriatric, hello geri-active

Is this you? A new survey from the Prudential puts over 55s in the picture

7.8 million over 55s want to become 'gap-year grannies and granddads' by travelling the world and taking more holidays.

8.0 million over 55s would like to eat out more frequently and socialise more often.

Nearly 1.3 million over 55s dream of writing a top-selling novel and 2.1 million intend to put their creative talents to good use by painting.

Baby-boomers are set to give bingo, bowls and knitting the flick in retirement.

However, when it comes to retirement, the big thing is still gardening.

New research from insurance company Prudential reveals that far from taking life at a slower pace when they retire, the baby-boomer generation plan to become 'geri-actives', busting the retirement clichés.

The research reveals that the over 55s are gearing up for an active retirement with the top six plans for 'life after work' being gardening, socialising, travelling, golf, painting and writing novels.

However, Prudential warns that the 'geri-active' dream has a price – those nearing retirement will have to find an extra £5,000 to fund this new lifestyle.

Greenfingers

Gardening tops the list of 'must do' activities for the over 55s, with over half (8.8 million) planning to spend more time in the great outdoors post-retirement. And more socialising is on the cards – eating out, visiting friends, dinner parties and spending more time in the pub are high on the agenda with 8.0 million over 55s

intending to step up their social lives once they give up work.

When it comes to sport, the over 55s are keen to get on the greens and perfect their swings with 1.6 million over 55s (three times as many men as women) planning to devote a lot of time to golf when they retire.

Globetrotters

The research also revealed that escaping to the sun and seeing the world will be a high priority for baby-boomers, perhaps inspired by the travel exploits of their children and grandchildren. 7.8 million over 55s would like to holiday and travel more once they retire, sparking a new trend of 'gap-year grannies and granddads'. And it's not necessarily a two-week jaunt we're talking about. Forty-five per cent of Brits have an appetite to live abroad permanently in retirement with the top five hotspots being Spain, Australia, France, Canada and USA.

Creative juices

It looks like these new horizons are also set to provide plenty of creative inspiration:

2.1 million over 55s plan to take up painting as a hobby in retirement.

Nearly one in ten – the equivalent of 1.3 million people – have aspirations to be the next 'blockbuster' author by penning a novel in retirement.

Perhaps surprisingly, crosswords and knitting, along with bingo and bowls, have been given the heave-ho.

Ali Crossley, Director for Prudential's Equity Release plans, comments: 'Many of the so-called baby-boomers will probably have seen their

children travel the world and enjoy many of the opportunities they weren't able to in their youth. Therefore in retirement they will be wanting to make up for lost time by enjoying new experiences and making the most of the "freedom" they've worked so hard for. The issue for many, however, is making sure they have the funds not only to live comfortably in retirement, but also the additional £5,000 or so needed to fulfil their new retirement lifestyle.

8.0 million over 55s would like to eat out more frequently and socialise more often

---

'A solution for some of these baby-boomers could be equity release. We estimate that the current generation of 50- to 60-year-olds have £570 billion equity in their homes and releasing some of this could provide them with that vital boost to their retirement income that they need to fulfil their dreams.'

For further information on the Prudential Home Equity Release Plan, visit www.pru.co.uk

Research was conducted by CIAR Consumer Omnibus amongst 576 non-retired adults and 268 adults aged 45+ retired or planning to retire in 2004.

■ The above information is from the LaterLife website which can be found at www.laterlife.com

© *LaterLife*.com

The fabulous fifty

Melody Stewart lists invaluable hints on slashing the risk of illness and increasing your chances of a long and happy life

1. **Nice guys die last** Doing good does you good, says a study in the journal *Psychology Science* that found that seniors who give emotional or practical support to others can reduce their risk of dying prematurely by as much as 60%, compared with those who don't.

2. **Eat less** A study of 19-month-old mice showed that those on 25% fewer calories a day lived 42% longer than their litter mates, while the journal *Proceedings of the National Academy of Sciences* reports that members aged 50-plus of the Calorie Restriction Optimal Nutrition Society were significantly healthier than a control group who consumed around 2,000 calories a day.

3. **Get the giggles** As well as releasing chemicals that relax blood vessels, laughing reduces levels of the stress hormones adrenalin and cortisol, increases pain-killing endorphins and provides as much of a circulation boost as aerobic exercise.

4. **Wholier than thou** Some 34,000 Iowa women who ate whole grains had a significantly lower death rate from all causes compared with women who eschewed them, says a University of Minnesota study.

5. **Floss** Did you know that inflammation-causing bacteria lurk in the tiny gaps between your teeth? Floss them away and reduce the risk of gum disease that can make you 72% more likely to suffer from heart disease, according to Harvard Medical School research.

6. **Veg out** A 22-year German study of a group of more than 2,000 vegetarians, vegans and occasional meat eaters found there were 41 fewer deaths per 100 in the group compared with the general population.

7. **Tuck into tuna** And anchovies, salmon and other oily fish – they boast omega-3 fatty acids linked to an 81% reduction in sudden male death, according to the *Journal of the American Medical Association*.

8. **Drink tea** The national drink appears to inhibit some of the brain chemicals associated with Alzheimer's disease, says the journal *Phytotherapy Research*. To reap the most benefits, swap black tea for green.

9. **Believe in something** Church attendance increases life expectancy, according to the *International Journal for Psychiatry and Medicine*. It helps to counter stress and emotional problems and appears to protect against heart, respiratory and digestive diseases.

10. **Berry good** Blueberries, cranberries, blackcurrants and tart cherries all boast high levels of antioxidants, the protective compounds that defend cells from damaging free radicals. Just 100g of blueberries a day can stimulate the growth of new brain cells and oxygenate the skin.

11. **Om** Do the 'Downward dog' and visualise your inner flame, because yoga and meditation get rid of stress-related killer chemicals, lower your blood pressure and strengthen the immune system.

12. **Get enough sleep** Fewer than five hours of sleep produces higher levels of a blood-clotting protein called fibrinogen that could slow blood flow to the brain and heart, but more than eight hours' sleep is linked to increased mortality levels.

13. **Enjoy a glass of red wine** Resveratrol, a compound found in red fruit skins, may play a role in fighting lung cancer and asthma. It also helps raise the levels of 'good' cholesterol and reduces platelet stickiness, helping to guard against the risk of heart disease and stroke.

14. **Live near a park** A study from Tokyo found that older people living near a green space live longer than people boxed in by concrete.

15. **Express yourself** Sing a song, write a journal, paint a picture – all are great ways of releasing pent-up emotions. According to the *Journal of Clinical Psychology*, people who write about their personal lives are healthier and make fewer visits to their doctors than those who don't.

16. **Grab a jab** Flu carries off many victims during the colder months.

Don't let it. Flu jabs are free to the over-65s, to people in nursing homes or old people's homes and to those with asthma, kidney disease, diabetes or a lowered immune system.

17. **Use it or lose it** Defend yourself against dementia by giving the brain a workout. While learning a language encourages the growth of grey matter, doing the crossword, reading or playing cards or board games was associated with a lower risk of dementia in adults aged over 75, according to a study published in the *New England Journal of Medicine*.

18. **Be bold** According to *New Scientist*, fearful rats have shorter lifespans than those more open to change. University of Chicago researchers linked fearfulness to protracted high levels of debilitating stress hormones.

19. **Dark delight** Chocolate containing large amounts of cocoa solids is actually good for you in small amounts, says a study from King's College London, which found that 50g contains as many antioxidising flavonoids as six apples, two glasses of wine or seven onions.

20. **Test your peepers** Eyes can offer clues to conditions such as diabetes and high blood pressure. Also, about a third of drivers can't see properly, so wearing glasses or contact lenses may reduce accident levels.

21. **Reduce salt** Sprinkling more on top of all the hidden salt in processed foods can raise blood pressure and put you at increased risk of heart disease and kidney failure.

22. **Stay married** It's worth working on your relationship. A study in the *Health Psychology Journal* showed that a long and happy marriage lengthens life expectancy, while divorce or remarrying can shorten it.

23. **Use your onion** Anything from the onion family, including garlic and leeks, is a good detoxifier as well as being antiseptic and antibacterial. Their sulphur compounds help protect against cancers and cardiovascular disease as well as strengthening bones.

Church attendance increases life expectancy, according to the International Journal for Psychiatry and Medicine

---

24. **Go to the dentist** This is the best person to examine your mouth for signs of oral cancers, so keep your date with the drill master.

25. **Eat breakfast** The University of Georgia Gerontology Center found that centenarians eat breakfast regularly.

26. **Dance to your own tune** A study by clinical psychologist Dr David Weeks suggests eccentricity is the key to a longer, happier life. Those who are untroubled by the norms of society suffer from much lower levels of stress, so their immune response systems function more efficiently.

27. **Good friends** Cultivate your social circle – an Ohio State University study found that students with adequate social support had a stronger immune system during exams than those without it.

28. **Stop smoking** No matter how late in life you give up, within five years your risk of a heart attack halves and after 10 years your risk level is the same as a person who has never smoked and your lung cancer risk also drops by 50%.

29. **Lemon aid** A warm cup of water with a squeeze of lemon juice helps stimulate the digestive system to remove toxins.

30. **Fall in love** Love is a great healer, says a Yale University study, which discovered fewer artery blockages in the hearts of people who felt well-loved. A healthy sex life can boost the immune system, burn calories and release pain-busting endorphins.

31. **Silver machine** Drivers of silver-coloured cars were 50% less likely to be seriously injured in a car crash than drivers of white vehicles, according to a New Zealand study of 1,000 drivers published in the *British Medical Journal*.

32. **Look on the bright side** Optimism is good for your health, say Dutch researchers. Their 10-year study of attitude and life expectancy found that positive thinkers reduced their risk of early death by 55%.

33. **Take control** Get involved with a club, volunteer at a local charity or take on tasks in the family – a study of 800 American retirees by the University of Michigan found that those who took on a valued role had significantly longer lives.

34. **Fat chance** Take a good look at the back of food packets – trans fats show up as hydrogenated vegetable oil and are implicated in cancer and heart disease. According to the *Archives of Neurology*, they may be linked to the development of dementia.

35. **Furry friends** In a study by the State University of New York, Buffalo, having a pet was so effective at reducing blood pressure that half the stockbrokers taking part in the study were able to quit medication. A study at Cambridge also found that pet-owners visited doctors less often.

36. **Culture is good for you** A nine-year Swedish study of 12,000 people, published in the *British Medical Journal*, found that people who visited galleries, theatres and concerts were 36% more likely to live longer, possibly because pleasure boosts the immune system.

37. **Weighty matters** Fat cells churn out hormones that increase the risk of heart disease and cancers of the colon, womb, gall bladder, ovaries and breast. According to the British Heart Foundation, more than 10% of heart attacks are due to obesity.

38. **Five alive** Make sure you get your five portions of fruit and veg a day, since a colourful plateful contains phytochemicals, antioxidants, vitamins, minerals and fibre.

39. **Play it safe** Leaving off your seatbelt, breaking the speed limit and missing check-ups are life-threatening in their own right, but apart from this, risk-taking behaviour raises damaging levels of stress.

40. **Don't party too hard** A couple of glasses of red wine (see 13) appears to have health benefits, but regularly glugging too much alcohol cripples the detoxifying organs like the liver and kidneys and puts you at risk of oral cancers.

41. **Eat an apple a day** It's more than an old wives' tale, according to French scientists. A type of antioxidant polyphenol called procyanidins, found in apples, has been shown to significantly reduce the number of pre-cancerous lesions in the colons of laboratory rats.

42. **Go nuts** A healthy snack, they provide omega 3 – essential fatty acids that the body can't produce. Brazil nuts top up supplies of anti-ageing selenium and almonds are an easy way to ingest vitamin E.

43. **Be saucy** Tomato-based sauces are brimming with lycopene – an antioxidant that helps stop cholesterol clinging to the walls of your arteries, and lycopene is easier for the body to absorb when found in heated tomatoes or tomato sauces.

44. **Do porridge** Get your oats, because the soluble fibre helps reduce blood cholesterol levels, while their high vitamin B content will help soothe stress levels.

45. **Move to Japan** According to the World Health Organisation, the Japanese lead longer, healthier lives than any other people, perhaps because of their traditionally low-fat diet. If that's too far away, France is third on the list while Britain limps in at 14.

46. **Exercise** Fitness is crucial throughout our lives, helping us halve heart disease risk, build bone strength and maintain balance to avoid life-threatening falls later in life.

47. **Tree of life** Make a list of family illnesses, as some, such as breast cancer and diabetes, can be inherited. You can then alert your own doctor and be on the lookout for telltale symptoms.

48. **Mediterranean magic** Olive oil helps protect against age-related disease with monounsaturated fats foiling bad cholesterol while protecting good cholesterol. Its antioxidants squalene and oleuropein also reduce the risk of cancers of the breast and the colon.

49. **Friendly bacteria** Live yoghurt helps populate your gut with armies of friendly bacteria that fight gastro-intestinal infections.

50. **Be a busy bee** According to Fred Hale, the world's oldest man who died in November at the age of 113, the recipe for a long life is a spoonful of pollen, another of honey, a short walk and a spot of gardening.

■ The above information is from the Here's Health section of *Saga Magazine* from February 2005, and was written by Melody Stewart. Visit the Saga website at www.saga.co.uk

© *Saga*

Forever young

With huge advances in genetic engineering, stem cell research and other technologies, it seems that ageing is a thing of the past. But, unless you can enjoy the best of health, would you want to stay young for ever? Liz Bestic reports

It seems as if every week we are bombarded with news of potions and pills that promise to 'hold back the ravages of time' and keep us forever young. Scientists seek the magic bullet that will stem the tide of ageing and provide us with that all-too-elusive elixir of life.

We are all aware that improved health care, better sanitation and good nutrition have helped us make dramatic strides in thwarting the forces which have shortened our lives.

The truth is that most of us would probably like to live longer if it meant that we could be healthy as well. Nobody wants to end up with the types of diseases which traditionally beset old age. Notching up the years just to live longer is no good if those years are marred by illnesses such as cancer, diabetes or heart disease. Our

hope is for a better, more youthful life that will go on longer, where quality of life is key.

Science may soon have means of slowing down our biological clocks and disrupting the mechanisms of ageing, and Cambridge biogerontologist Dr Aubrey de Grey suggests that a breakthrough could be just around the corner.

'I believe that we have a 50-50 chance of developing a human rejuvenation therapy that works within 10 to 15 years,' he says.

Dr de Grey's opinions may seem controversial, yet many of his colleagues still believe that the ability to postpone ageing is close at hand.

'Most scientists accept the principle that we have the technical expertise to apply the biotechnological tools to postpone ageing. However, to do that sooner rather than later would take billions of pounds and a load of political goodwill. There is a school of thought which believes that ageing is inevitable and because all of us have to put up with it, sometimes it is easier simply to invent idiotic excuses for why it might actually be a good thing,' he says.

'We won't be able to eliminate heart disease, stroke and cancer, but we will develop therapies to knock them back repeatedly and restore the individual to a healthy life.'

Scientists have been beavering away behind the scenes for years to find out what makes humans age, by looking at all sorts of unlikely species such as roundworms, fruit-flies and monkeys. Researchers in the US, for example, have bred mutant worms which can live for up to 120 days – six times their normal lifespan and the equivalent of 500 years in human terms.

'By changing a few genes it has been possible to keep these worms alive and youthful for much longer,' explains Michael Rose of the University of California.

Treatments have also been discovered which can make human cells grown in vitro last for ever. They have discovered diet regimes which can increase the lifespan of mice while making them healthier.

'We are undergoing a major scientific revolution in our understanding of ageing,' says Dr de Grey.

The DNA connection

A main key to the ageing process is telomeres – the little bits of DNA sequences which protect the ends of our chromosomes. These are the vital components which are keeping those cells alive in the culture dishes in laboratories. Scientists who have grown connective tissue cells in culture have discovered that telomeres get shorter and shorter each time the cells divide. When the telomeres are really short, they release an enzyme called telomerase which rebuilds telomeres, effectively rendering the cells immortal.

Our hope is for a better, more youthful life that will go on longer, where quality of life is key

---

Meanwhile, in laboratory experiments researchers have generated mice with no telomerase and discovered that, as the animals age, their telomeres shrink, but they do not develop any of the illnesses generally associated with ageing, such as cataracts, osteoporosis and cardiac disease. It is hoped that in the future, by using telomerase in the right cells, scientists may be able to boost immune function or strengthen bone and skin.

Factors involved in ageing

So now we know that telomerase is an important factor in ageing, but still scientists are not sure exactly how it works.

Most believe that ageing is the result of more than just one factor anyway. Free radicals which attack our DNA are big culprits because they can damage almost every critical component of our cells. Oxygen is toxic and the rate at which we age may well be the result of how well our bodies can actually detoxify these oxygen radicals.

Free radicals may be the reason why, for example, pigeons can live for 35 years – 12 times as long as rats, which are about the same size. For the amount of oxygen they take in, pigeons produce half as many free radicals as rodents do.

Recently, Professor John Speakman of the University of Aberdeen has discovered a compound called UCP3, which reduces production of free radicals.

'If we could bottle this substance we could be looking at a drug in 10 to 20 years' time which could truly keep us young well into old age,' he says.

Insulin has also been isolated as an important component in the ageing process. Investigations into those worms that live six times as long as average show that they respond differently to hormones such as insulin. Animals that burn glucose more efficiently – extracting more energy from less blood sugar – somehow manage to live longer and healthier lives.

Researchers have latched on to this as a possible way of developing therapies aimed at manipulating hormones which may be able to put the brakes on ageing. At the very least, they hope these types of therapies may stave off age-related diseases, such as osteoporosis, muscle loss, heart disease and cancer.

Calorie restriction is also known to have some effect on the ageing process.

Mice and rats on a diet high in protein but low in calories live about 30% to 60% longer than their counterparts that are on high-calorie diets – and they are healthier, too. We also know that certain monkeys have low insulin levels, can regulate their glucose better and have far less free radical damage to their skeletal muscles. This raises the possibility that therapies aimed at manipulating hormones might put the brakes on ageing.

As Judith Campisi of America's Lawrence Berkeley National Laboratory explains:

'It would be hard for people to starve themselves so that they could live to be 150, and difficult to cut so many calories and still maintain proper nutrition. But if we can catalogue the physiological changes that occur in animals, we may be able to find a drug which accomplishes the same thing in humans.'

Growing new body parts

What of stem cell research? If you think the possibility of growing new body parts is merely a flight of fancy, think again.

If you cut off a newt's leg, it grows back weeks later, so why is it so hard for us to imagine humans regenerating body parts in the same way?

Very young children can regrow their fingertips even up to the first knuckle and, recently in the UK, cells have been harvested from small pieces of healthy cartilage that has been extracted from damaged knee-joints, cultured and then implanted back into the patient's knees in a procedure which could make knee replacements redundant.

In the next decades, regeneration may allow doctors to repair hearts, livers, skin and even injured spinal cords. Christopher Reeve, the American actor who, sadly, died last month, believed passionately in this type of treatment.

Food makes a difference

It is true that the science of ageing has come on in leaps and bounds over the past 30 years or so. But how does any of this affect us now and is there anything we can be doing to ensure a longer and healthier life?

The short answer is yes. We all know there are certain foods we should avoid if we want to live a healthier life – cutting out saturated fat and eating more fruit and vegetables is a good start. However, there is now clear evidence that some foods can help prevent the wear and tear on cells which causes cancer,

---

While some see ageing as an unavoidable process where a decline can only be 'managed', others define it as a specific biological process which, one day, we may learn how to switch off

---

diabetes, stroke and heart disease. They can even prevent other signs of ageing, such as wrinkles.

An American study of 1,300 elderly people showed that those who ate two or more portions a day of dark-pigmented vegetables, such as kale or spinach, were only half as likely to suffer a heart attack and had a third of the risk of dying of cancer compared with people eating an average of less than one portion a day.

Research also shows there is another group of foods which may counter ageing. Oily fish, such as salmon, mackerel, herring and sardines, all contain high levels of essential fatty acids or omega oils which can lower heart disease rates and help other chronic age-related conditions, such as osteoarthritis. These oils can also help the skin to stay clear and wrinkle-free, partly because they also contain high levels of vitamin A.

More importantly, they also keep the brain young. Animal experiments have shown that if the brain is deprived of omega oils, memory function may be impaired. A US

study on rats showed that after four months of finding their way around a maze, those that were deprived of omega oils had lower brain function and higher blood pressure and began to get lost. Six months later, their memory had badly deteriorated.

One of the major barriers to finding a solution to the problem of ageing is the scientific establishment's failure to agree on what ageing really is.

While some see it as an unavoidable process where a decline can only be 'managed', others define it as a specific biological process which, one day, we may learn how to switch off.

Dr de Grey and his supporters are happy to shake up the traditional approaches to old age.

'Most of us only think there is anything wrong with "curing" ageing because we have grown up with the notion that it is ghastly but inevitable.

'We may not be able to eliminate deadly diseases from the body, but we will be able to have periodic treatments to knock them back. People will simply go back for rejuvenation every few years,' he explains.

'I do predict that an ageing population of baby boomers will soon put unprecedented pressure on politicians to deliver properly-funded research into life extension. Then all ethical objections will be shown to be, quite simply, a smokescreen.'

■ The above information is from *The Lady* magazine's website which can be found at www.lady.co.uk

© *The Lady*

LIVE FOR JUST ABOUT EVER?! .... WISH I'D BEEN BORN A HEDONIST...

Seniors kiss 'Hello' lifestyle goodbye

Information from the Association of Retired and Persons over 50

Older people are more on the ball when it comes to enjoying their own lives and spending their own money than they are living vicariously through articles about David Beckham and other celebrities in glossy magazines, according to a survey of its 50,000 members undertaken by the Association of Retired and Persons Over 50 (ARP/O50).

In the opinion of 92 per cent, 'society wastes the experience of older people'

Staying informed
It was essential, said 88 per cent of respondents, to 'make an effort to keep up to date with what's going on in the world' and 54 per cent felt 'better informed' than ever before, with magazine articles on personal finance, travel and humour favoured over celebrity interviews and fashion features.

Money matters
With their mortgages behind them and the kids' university fees paid, 57 per cent admitted to being 'better off than ever' but many – 78 per cent – complained that the threshold of Inheritance Tax was still 'far too low'. A lower tax threshold for pensioners was advocated (by 81 per cent) along with a higher basic universal pension and no means testing (78 per cent).

Universal concerns
Better NHS provision was prominent among seniors' other demands, ranking alongside concerns about immigration, the environment, crime, terrorism and the controversial closure of local post offices.

There was also majority agreement (83 per cent) that seniors' travel and other concessions should be applied uniformly 'throughout the UK'.

Happy – despite reservations about government
Despite the feeling that 'governments are less trustworthy than they used to be' (a view shared by 69 per cent), 78 per cent remained 'very' or 'quite' happy with life in general (down by 16 per cent since 2001), the primary caveat being that 44 per cent 'would have liked to make a greater financial provision for my retirement'.

Undervalued and marginalised
But, in the opinion of 92 per cent, 'society wastes the experience of older people' and 85 per cent felt that society too often marginalised older people.

Comment by ARP/O50's Director of Social Policy
Commenting on the survey, ARP/O50's Director of Social Policy, Don Steele, said: 'The findings accurately reflect the concerns and lifestyles of Britain's 20 million over fifties who, although feeling marginalised by the mainstream media, advertisers and suppliers, continue to enjoy active and fulfilling lives in retirement.

'In spite of their enormous potential spending power, seniors still face rejection by some store card and other credit providers as they get older. This is just another area (like discrimination in employment and NHS provision) of which many younger people remain unaware and politicians choose to ignore. The survey stands as an important reminder to society of the age-based inequalities that still exist and the need to level the playing field by changing outdated attitudes towards age and creating a more positive attitude to older people and the ageing process.'

■ Information from the Association of Retired and Persons over 50 – visit www.arp050.org.uk or see page 41 for address details.

© ARP050

Our good old days

We're staying younger longer. And that's reason to celebrate

By Tom Kirkwood

We are all in for a shock. It's not bad news. In fact, it's the best news possible. People are living longer. Even good news is disturbing, though, when we are unprepared. And our species is about as unprepared for the longevity revolution as the dinosaurs were for the arrival of mammals. As a result, mankind's greatest triumph – a more than doubling in life expectancy over just eight generations – might very easily turn sour.

The increase in longevity should not be a surprise; it's been going on for 200 years. Life expectancy within the UK has been increasing by two years a decade for as long as any of us can recall. That means that for each hour that passes, life expectancy increases by 12 minutes.

So why have governments not seen the longevity revolution coming? Why have they not made the gentle adjustments to our course that would steer the ships of state smoothly towards a world where we all live so much longer and enjoy better health and vitality in old age? The answer lies in a combination of short-termism and denial.

Short-termism is a problem for governments, particularly those which rely on democratic re-election. As we know from the failure to address climate change, processes that occur gradually over decades tend to be poorly addressed by governments which must account for their actions every few years.

But it is denial that underlies our inertia about ageing. None of us likes to think about ageing when we are young, and that goes for opinion-formers and politicians. By the time we are ready to address it, our influence tends to be on the wane. Such denial nourishes the ageism that pervades society. Old age is overwhelmingly seen as a time of loss – of teeth, of hair, of speed of thought, of vigour, of sexuality. But for most people, the reality of ageing can also be a process of growth, bringing satisfaction and self-knowledge.

A key element of the traditional view of ageing has been that the processes leading to frailty, disease and death were somehow programmed into us as a fixed feature of our biological make-up. It was this idea that led the UN in 1980, and again in 1990, to forecast a flattening out of the increase in longevity, forecasts that have proved spectacularly wrong.

The idea was that once the gains that had been made from controlling early mortality, mainly by improved sanitation, vaccination and antibiotics, had run their course, we should find ourselves left with the fixed, ineluctable reality of ageing. But the past 20 years have seen no slowing of the lifespan increase. This is being driven now by declining death rates among the oldest age groups of the population. We are reaching old age in better shape than ever before.

> *Our species is about as unprepared for the longevity revolution as the dinosaurs were for the arrival of mammals*

There is no genetic programme for ageing. Science has revealed that we age not because some inner clock tells us to but because the biological systems that keep us going, by repairing all the little faults in our cells and tissues, were set for an era when the chances were that you would not live much longer than 30 or 40 years...an accident or infection would get you first. Our bodies are programmed not for death but for survival, but we live with repair

HAPPY BIRTHDAY GRANDSON!

systems that suited our ancestors, in their more dangerous environment, much better than they suit us today, when we have made our lives so very much safer. Eventually, the damage builds to a level that proves our undoing.

We can do a lot to improve our chances of healthier ageing, through choices on lifestyle and nutrition

---

This explains why there is no fixed limit to human longevity. The current world record of 122 years and five months will be broken. It probably also explains why we are reaching old age in better shape. The kinder conditions of modern life mean that our bodies experience less damage. And we can do a lot to improve our chances of healthier ageing, through choices on lifestyle and nutrition. One of the stark injustices in today's Britain is the 10-year difference in life expectancy between the shortest and longest living regions.

Certainly there are challenges ahead as lives lengthen. Pensions, for example, need a radical rethink. Retirement at 65 was introduced a century ago when average life span was 10 years or more before retiring age. It is now about 15 years beyond it. It is small wonder then that the system is feeling the strain and we may need to work longer. But is this really so dreadful, so long as it is introduced fairly? We enjoy longer lives and better health than our

grandparents, and continuing in work gives you a better income than most pensions.

The building of a society that celebrates age is not an act of charity. Combating ageism and its ills is not about 'them and us'- it's 'us and us'. You will be old too. Bend the ears of politicians now and we will all share the benefits. We owe it not only to ourselves but to the generations before us, who fought to overcome the scourge of early death so that we now enjoy the right to become old.

■ Tom Kirkwood is co-director of the Institute for Ageing and Health at the University of Newcastle upon Tyne. His books include *The End of Age*, based on his BBC Reith Lectures.
This article first appeared in *The Observer* on 3 April 2005.
© *Guardian Newspapers Limited 2005*

Over-80s will double to 5 million in a generation

By Sarah Womack, Social Affairs Correspondent

The number of people living to 80 and beyond will double within 30 years to almost five million, according to a study released yesterday (28 July 2004).

By the early 2050s, the 80-plus population will peak at close to seven million, says the Office for National Statistics. By that time the population as a whole will be about 65 million.

Help the Aged said the figures emphasised the need for the Government to tackle age discrimination and abolish the compulsory retirement age. Andrea Lane, a spokesman, said: 'These statistics map out the vital role the older population will play in our society and particularly in the workplace.'

The figures show that the number of older people overall will increase 'significantly', with the population's average age rising from 39.3 in 2002 to 43.6 in 2031.

The number of children is expected to fall from 11.8 million in 2002 to just below 11 million in 2014, resulting in the working population becoming much older. The 45-59 age group will increase by 15 per cent by 2018 while the number of adults under 30 will fall from 13.5 million to 11.9 million by 2017.

The Society of Financial Advisers said people faced a bleak retirement because they underestimated their life expectancy by an average of 5.3 years.

Its research, carried out with the Institute of Actuaries and the Continuing Mortality Investigation Bureau, found that women aged 25-34 underestimated their life expectancy by 6.5 years. They expected to live until they were just over 82 rather than 89.

Men were only slightly better at judging how long they would live, expecting to die 5.1 years earlier than actuaries are predicting – at 82 rather than 87.

Women over 55 were even more likely to underestimate life expectancy, underestimating by seven years the 88 years they are likely to live. Men over 55 were slightly better, getting to within 2.2 years of their 85 expected years.

Bob Bullivant, the managing director of Sofa, said: 'It is a disaster quietly bubbling under, but it is timed to explode in years to come as today's workforce realises it has short-changed itself in making appropriate provision for a long retirement.'

© *Telegraph Group Limited, London 2004*

Adults in later life with mental health problems

Information from the Mental Health Foundation

Facts and figures

It is estimated that 18% of the general population in the UK are of pensionable age and that this figure will grow to 20% by 2025. As a society, we tend to assume that older people will develop mental health problems as a 'normal' aspect of ageing. Most older people do not develop mental health problems, although a significant minority does. For example:

- about 25% of people over 85 have dementia.
- between 10 and 15% of people over 65 have depression.
- between 4 and 23% of older adults seen by medical staff have an alcohol problem.

In addition to those older people who have an identifiable mental illness such as dementia, there are many who experience psychological or emotional distress associated with isolation, loneliness or loss. These problems are not recorded by the health or medical care system.

What problems affect people in later life?

Dementia

Dementia is a decline in mental ability which affects memory, thinking, problem solving, concentration, perception and behaviour. Some forms of dementia, such as Alzheimer's disease, are degenerative. That is, they get worse over time. Other forms of dementia, such as vascular dementia, may be non-degenerative. That is, they may not get worse over time.

People with dementia can become confused. Some people also become restless or display repetitive behaviour. They may also seem irritable, tearful or agitated. This can be very distressing for both the person with dementia and their family and friends. Some people with dementia also develop other problems such as

> *About one in 20 people over the age of 65 are affected by dementia and this figure rises to one in four people over the age of 85*

depression, disturbed sleep, aggression, inappropriate sexual behaviour and incontinence, although the latter issues tend to be associated with more advanced dementia.

About one in 20 people over the age of 65 are affected by dementia and this figure rises to one in four people over the age of 85 (Audit Commission, 2000). People under the age of 65 can develop dementia but this is rare and is known as early onset or pre-senile dementia.

What causes dementia?

Dementia occurs as a result of the death of brain cells or damage in parts of the brain that deal with our thought processes and functioning. The most common form of dementia is Alzheimer's disease. We do not know what causes Alzheimer's disease but we do know that ageing is the biggest risk factor. The second most common type of dementia is vascular or multi-infarct dementia. This occurs as a result of a series of mini-strokes which constrict blood flow and oxygen to the brain.

Can it be prevented and is there a cure?

Most types of dementia cannot be cured but a number of psychological treatments and anti-dementia drugs can be very effective for those in the early stages of dementia. It is therefore very important to get a proper assessment of cognitive function from a medical practitioner as early as possible.

There are no guaranteed ways of preventing dementia, but you may find it helpful to follow a sensible diet and pursue a healthy lifestyle. Regular physical exercise and supplements like Gingko Biloba can help to ensure that there is always a good supply of blood to the brain. Please consult your GP before taking such medication. You can also help yourself by keeping your mind active, for example by doing crosswords or puzzles.

For more detailed information please see *Dementia Factsheet – Mental Health Foundation, 2000.*

Depression

Depression describes a range of moods, from feeling a bit low to a severe problem, which interferes with everyday life and normal functioning. People with severe depression may experience a range of symptoms including low mood, loss of interest and pleasure as well as feelings of worthlessness or guilt.

It is estimated that around 10-15% of elderly people in the community exhibit depressive symptoms

---

Depression can affect anyone, of any culture, age or background but it affects proportionally more older people than any other age group. It is estimated that around 10-15% of elderly people in the community exhibit depressive symptoms, with this proportion rising to about 40% of care home residents (Baldwin, 2002). That said, you will not necessarily become depressed just because you are getting older.

What causes depression?

There are a number of risk factors that play a role in increasing older people's vulnerability to depression including:

- being widowed, divorced or retired
- neurobiological changes associated with ageing
- use of medication for other conditions
- greater physical impairment and disease
- loneliness and isolation
- genetic susceptibility, which increases with age.

Can it be prevented and is there a cure?

Depression in later life is a widely under-recognised and under-treated medical condition. Up until recently many health professionals – including GPs – failed to offer the treatments and supports available to other age groups. Most forms of depression can be treated, using medication, talking treatments or other strategies.

It can be difficult to diagnose depression in older people because it often occurs alongside other mental and physical illnesses, such as dementia, stroke, diabetes and cancer. In addition many older people do not seek help from their GP until they have a number of symptoms. As with dementia, it is important to seek help as early as possible.

Self-help strategies that can help reduce the risk of depression include:

- taking regular exercise
- planning for critical transitions such as retirement

- seeking support from family and friends following the loss of a long-term partner
- ensuring that you pursue a range of interests in later life.

For more detailed information please see *Depression Factsheet – Mental Health Foundation, 2000.*

Dementia and depression

The relationship between dementia and depression is complex. The symptoms of dementia and depression – including withdrawal from social activities and general apathy – are very similar. An elderly person with severe depression may occasionally be misdiagnosed as having dementia. A person with dementia may also become depressed.

Alcohol abuse

It is estimated that between 4% and 23% of older adults seen by medical staff experience problems with alcohol. Figures also show that older men are currently between two and six times more likely than older women to be at risk of abusing alcohol.

Although alcohol abuse is a problem for people of all ages, it is more likely to go unrecognised among older people. Many older people use alcohol to deal with loss or loneliness. Approximately 10-30% of older people who abuse alcohol become depressed. They are also at greater risk of suicide (Atkinson, 2002).

For more detailed information about alcohol abuse, please see *Alcoholism and Alcohol Abuse Factsheet – Mental Health Foundation, 2003.*

Medication

Prescribed medications can cause mental health difficulties among older people. A recent Department of Health survey found that 79% of older people take prescribed medicines. Many older people take four or more medications at the same time. There are risks associated with taking multiple medications, including confusion (Department of Health, 2001).

More detailed information about medication and mental health problems can be found at the following websites:

...TIME TO GET MOVING!

SK

- *Medication for Mental Health Problems Factsheet* – Mental Health Foundation, 2000.
- The Medicines and Drugs section on the *Mental Health in Later Life* website (http://www.mhilli.org/medicines/index.html)

Other mental health problems

There are a number of rarer mental health problems that affect older people, including delirium, anxiety and late-onset schizophrenia. The prevalence, nature, and course of these disorders are different in older people, as are the treatments that may be offered. For more detailed information please see our *Anxiety* and *Schizophrenia* factsheets.

Capacity and older people with mental illness

People with dementia or severe mental illness may have difficulty in making and communicating decisions. Very few people are unable to be involved in making choices at all but some may have partial or fluctuating mental capacity and may need help with communication. Different approaches are also required to engage a person with dementia. They often need longer to make decisions, may need an advocate to speak on their behalf and their mental functioning may also vary by day, and time of day. Family members or carers are often useful sources of information but it is important to take account of the views of the person with dementia alongside those of their carer.

For more information about capacity please visit the Making Decisions Alliance website at www.makingdecisions.org.uk

Government initiatives

The promotion of good mental health is as important for older people as it is for younger people and has been recognised as a legal duty in Standard 8 of the National Service Framework for Older People (Department of Health, 2001).

Recent policy responses to meeting the mental health needs of older people also include two Audit Commission (2000, 2002) reports on mental health services for older people.

Help for carers

Caring for an older person with mental health problems can be very stressful, time consuming and emotionally and physically challenging. Caring for an older person with dementia is associated with higher levels of stress, with a third of carers suffering from depression (Milne et al., 2001).

Please see *Carers of people with mental health problems – a select list of resources* – Mental Health Foundation, 2000 for more information and details of organisations that can help advise and support carers.

■ The above information is reprinted with kind permission from the Mental Health Foundation – for more information, please visit www.mentalhealth.org.uk or if you would like to write to them please see page 41 for address details.

© The Mental Health Foundation.

Does religion protect the elderly from depression?

A new study from Ireland suggests that attending church may protect elderly people from depression

Religious institutions are the most widely available social organisations for the elderly. Studies from the USA have suggested an inverse relationship between religiosity and late-life depression. Older Irish people have probably the highest levels of church attendance in Europe. The aims of this study were to describe patterns of church attendance among Irish people living in the community; to explore associated demographic factors; and to describe the relationship between mental and physical health and church attendance.

1462 people aged 65 and over completed an interview designed to diagnose depression. 133 were found to be depressed, and were compared with a control group of healthy subjects.

Religious denomination and frequency of church attendance were assessed, and sociodemographic information collected. Additional information about physical health and life-events was obtained from the group with depression.

It was found that 97% of the subjects were Roman Catholic. 77.9% attended church regularly; 14.7% were non-attenders; and 7.4% were occasional attenders.

Regular church attendance was significantly positively associated with belonging to a social network at low risk of depression. Being single was negatively associated with depression and with advancing age.

Analysis of both groups showed that those who attended church regularly were more likely to report distressing health problems, but less likely to be depressed or to have a number of chronic medical conditions.

■ The above information is from the Royal College of Psychiatrists' website which can be found at www.rcpsych.ac.uk, or see page 41.

© 2004 Royal College of Psychiatrists

- After years of studying ageing, Professor Tom Kirkwood realised that we age because only our genes need to survive. The rest of us is disposable. (page 1)

- In 2003, 6,433 women and 6,283 men were between 45 and 64, the highest figure for any age group. (page 2)

- There is growing evidence that women are biologically tougher than men. For example, we now know that female hormones protect women from heart disease, at least until the menopause. The reasons for women's biological resilience have to do with the way we have all evolved to play our reproductive roles. (page 2)

- The number of people over pensionable age, taking account of the change in the women's retirement age, is projected to increase from nearly 11.4 million in 2006 to 12.2 million in 2011, and will rise to nearly 13.9 million by 2026, reaching over 15.2 million in 2031. (page 4)

- For almost half of men over 50, music is still an important part of life. Amazingly at this stage in life, men are just as likely to go to pop and rock concerts as they are to go to classical music concerts and recitals (15%). (page 6)

- 1.28 million (14 per cent) older people in the UK regularly feel lonely. (page 12)

- One in ten (11 per cent) of older people see their grandchildren less than twice a year; 19 per cent of those who live alone will go more than a month without seeing any members of their family, and 9 per cent will go more than six months. (page 12)

- Abuse of older people generally happens within a relationship. It is a single or repeated act or lack of appropriate action that is done to the older person by someone such as a relative, carer, neighbour or a member of staff at a care home or day centre. (page 13)

- A project funded by the Economic and Social Research Council identified that 'being oneself', and feeling positive about it, enabled older people who can no longer live at home to enjoy a better quality of life. (page 15)

- Currently arbitrary age barriers mean older citizens can't participate in many voluntary and civic activities, such as being a magistrate after a particular birthday. (page 17)

- Although there is no legislation at present on age discrimination in employment in the UK the UK Government has committed to the EU Directive to introduce age discrimination legislation by December 2006. (page 18)

- By 2021 there will be more people over 80 than there are children under 5. (page 19)

- Currently around one-third of people between the ages of 50 and state pension age are not working. (page 19)

- Those in their sixties are more confident and happy to work than is typically believed, with 93 per cent saying they like their jobs. (page 23)

- Age directly links with sex, with women more likely than men to have been put off applying for a job because of age. (page 23)

- 25 per cent of school leavers have faced age discrimination compared to 21 per cent of those over 50 and 18% of those over 60. (page 24)

- The UK is the world's fourth richest country yet more than two million pensioners live below the poverty line. The older you are the greater your chances of living in poverty. (page 25)

- The UK, like most developed western countries, faces a demographic time bomb. The UK's ageing population means that in the not too distant future there will be too few workers to pay the pensions of older people. (page 26)

- The accumulated knowledge, experience and easier access to finance means that the average 50-year-old setting up a business can expect that business to last twice as long as an average 20-year-old's business – 5 years instead of 2.5 years. (page 27)

- 7.8 million over 55s want to become 'gap-year grannies and granddads' by travelling the world and taking more holidays. (page 28)

- In the opinion of 92 per cent of over-50s surveyed, 'society wastes the experience of older people' and 85 per cent felt that society too often marginalised older people. (page 34)

- For each hour that passes, life expectancy increases by 12 minutes. (page 35)

- The number of people living to 80 and beyond will double within 30 years to almost five million. (page 36)

- About 25% of people over 85 have dementia. Between 10 and 15% of people over 65 have depression. (page 37)

- 79% of older people take prescribed medicines, some taking four or more at once. (page 38)

ADDITIONAL RESOURCES

You might like to contact the following organisations for further information. Due to the increasing cost of postage, many organisations cannot respond to enquiries unless they receive a stamped, addressed envelope.

Age Concern England
Astral House
1268 London Road
LONDON SW16 4ER
Tel: 020 8765 7200
Email: ace@ace.org.uk
Website: www.ageconcern.org.uk
Age Concern supports all people over 50 in the UK. We provide essential services such as day care and information. We campaign on issues like age discrimination and pensions, and work to influence public opinion and government policy about older people.
To obtain written information such as money, legal issues, health, community care and housing, telephone their information line on Freephone 0800 009966 open 7 days a week, 7am to 7pm.

Age Positive
Department for Work and Pensions
Room W8d, Moorfoot
SHEFFIELD S1 4PQ
Email: agepositive@geronimopr.com
Website: www.agepositive.gov.uk
The Age Positive campaign promotes the benefits of employing a mixed-age workforce that includes older and younger people. We encourage employers to make decisions about recruitment, training and retention that do not discriminate against someone because of their age.

ARP/050 – The Association of Retired and Persons over 50
Windsor House
1270 London Road
LONDON SW16 4DH
Tel: 020 8764 3344
Email: info@arp.org.uk
Website: www.arp050.org.uk
Works to change the attitude towards age of individuals and society as a whole so as to enhance the quality of life for the over 50s, both present and future. Publishes ARP 050, a magazine for the retired.

Chartered Institute of Personnel and Development (CIPD)
151 The Broadway
Wimbledon
LONDON SW19 1JQ
Tel: 020 8971 9000
Email: ipd@cipd.co.uk
Website: www.cipd.co.uk
With over 105,000 members it is the professional body for those involved in the management and development of people.

Counsel and Care
Twyman House
16 Bonny Street
LONDON NW1 9PG
Tel: 020 7241 8555
Email: advice@counselandcare.org.uk
Website: www.counselandcare.org.uk
Counsel and Care's vision is for a society where older people are valued and respected, where they have choice and control over their lives and when they need help, our vision is for it to be delivered in an appropriate, flexible and supportive way. Advice Line: Local rate 0845 300 7585. (10 a.m.-12.30 p.m. and 2-4 p.m.)

Economic and Social Research Council (ESRC)
Polaris House
North Star Avenue
SWINDON
Wiltshire SN2 1UJ
Tel: 01793 413000
Email: exrel@esrc.ac.uk
Website: www.esrc.ac.uk
The ESRC is the UK's largest independent funding agency for research and postgraduate training into social and economic issues.

Help the Aged
207-221 Pentonville Road
LONDON N1 9UZ
Tel: 020 7278 1114
Email: info@helptheaged.org.uk
Website: www.helptheaged.org.uk
Help the Aged is working hard for a world in which older people are valued for their contribution to society, involved in their local communities and fulfilled in their needs, hopes and aspirations. They publish useful factsheets and leaflets.

Mental Health Foundation
Sea Containers House
20 Upper Ground
LONDON SE1 9QB
Tel: 020 78031 100
Email: mhf@mhf.org.uk
Website: www.mentalhealth.org.uk
The Mental Health Foundation is the leading UK charity working in mental health and learning disabilities. It exists to help people survive, recover from and prevent mental health problems.

Royal College of Psychiatrists
17 Belgrave Square
LONDON SW1X 8PG
Tel: 020 7235 2351
Email: rcpsych@rcpsych.ac.uk
Website: www.rcpsych.ac.uk
Improving the lives of people affected by mental illness. Produces an excellent series of free leaflets on various aspects of mental health.

The Work Foundation (formerly The Industrial Society)
Customer Centre
Quadrant Court
49 Calthorpe Road
Edgbaston
BIRMINGHAM B15 1TH
Tel: 0870 165 6700
Email: contact@theworkfoundation.com
Website: www.theworkfoundation.com
The Work Foundation is an independent, not-for-profit thinktank and consultancy. Through research, campaigning and practical interventions, we aim to improve the productivity and the quality of working life in the UK.

INDEX

ACKNOWLEDGEMENTS

The publisher is grateful for permission to reproduce the following material.

While every care has been taken to trace and acknowledge copyright, the publisher tenders its apology for any accidental infringement or where copyright has proved untraceable. The publisher would be pleased to come to a suitable arrangement in any such case with the rightful owner.

Chapter One: Ageing Trends

Ageing, © Help the Aged, Older people in the United Kingdom, © Age Concern, Male over fifties, reliving the swinging sixties, © Mintel, The young worry more about getting older, © DeHavilland Information Services Plc, The gender gap, © Saga, New phones help to keep elderly mobile, © Telegraph Group Ltd, London 2005, Grandparents caught by the web, © DeHavilland Information Services Plc, Britain's old and lonely, © Help the Aged, Older people at risk of abuse, © Counsel and Care, Older people in care homes, © ESRC.

Chapter Two: Ageism and Employment

Age – a relevant value?, © Communigate, Ageism, © Seniors Network 2004, Legislation on age discrimination, © University of Westminster, Flexible working in an ageing society, © Flexibility, Discrimination against older women, © Liverpool John Moores University, 90 not out, © 2005 Associated Newspapers Ltd, Why sixty is the new forte, © CIPD,

Age discrimination hits young people too, © Crown Copyright is reproduced with the permission of Her Majesty's Stationery Office, What is the pensions crisis?, © Help the Aged, Money talk, © TAEN 2004, UK employers must retain 50+ workers, © The Work Foundation.

Chapter Three: Ageing and Health

Goodbye geriatric, hello geri-active, © LaterLife.com, The fabulous fifty, © Saga, Forever young, © The Lady, Seniors kiss 'Hello' lifestyle goodbye, © ARP050, Our good old days, © Guardian Newspapers Limited 2005, Over-80s will double to 5 million in a generation, © Telegraph Group Ltd, London 2004, Adults in later life with mental health problems, © The Mental Health Foundation, Does religion protect the elderly from depression?, © 2004 Royal College of Psychiatrists.

Photographs and illustrations:

Pages 1, 15, 37: Don Hatcher; pages 2, 35: Angelo Madrid; pages 7, 14, 17, 33, 38: Simon Kneebone; pages 11, 29: Pumpkin House; pages 16, 21, 34: Bev Aisbett.

Craig Donnellan
Cambridge
September, 2005